What is the one thing we can take with us into eternity? People. What could be more important than reaching young people for Christ? Nothing. ... est challenge. So read Co... let my friend Sean Dun... his most urgent of all mi... of Jesus and the life-cha...

— **Mark Mittelberg**, International speaker and author of the Contagious Faith book and training course

Sean is a man on a mission. *Contending for the Rising Generations* is Sean's life calling, hands down. Reaching today's young adults with the love of Christ, realizing MILLIONS of professions of faith, is truly a game changer for the kingdom. I'm grateful for Sean, our friendship, and the opportunity to "run together" to fulfill and advance The Great Commission. An amazing journey!

— **Steve Kaloper**, The "DoingGoodBetter" Guy

Do you know someone who is under the age of 40? How about under 30? Chances are they're facing tough times. Many in the Millennial and Gen Z generations need hope right now. The real-life stories, stats and wisdom in Contending for the Rising Generations blew my mind and gave me great HOPE for our world. These are priceless, God-inspired insights and learnings for a time such as this. Please read and share this book right now!

— **Dr. Jim Bechtold**, Chief IMPACT Officer, CEO Forum; Former Marketing, Strategy, and Planning Leader, P&G North America; Vice Chair, World Vision US Board of Directors

Sean Dunn and his team connect digitally with millions of our young "struggling to survive" generation per week. In this book Sean helps us understand the "living in chaos" hearts and minds of our children, grandchildren, nieces, nephews, neighbors, and even strangers. Then, he shares hundreds of wise and proven insights on how to be an ever more effective bridge connecting this "lost" generation with our loving heavenly father. If you have been begging God to help you connect effectively with the young ones you love so deeply, this book has been written for you!

– **Bobb Biehl**, Executive Mentor, Author, Scottsdale, Arizona

Contending for the Rising Generations is much more than words on a page. Sean has penned a passionate plea and clarion call for us to see the next generations' struggles, and presents a compelling call to action to bring them hope. Gripped with the understanding that the younger generations don't respect religious form and ritual, Sean shows how to have an authentic encounter through meaningful conversations and how to engage the next generations in relationship with the real Jesus of the gospels. This book is filled with real-life, practical examples that will challenge your thinking about how you can be part of "The Army of Ordinaries" to win the battle for our young people. As Sean reminds us, we must live as if lives depend on us because they do. You will appreciate the tools and wisdom he shares, not from theory but from life experience. L.E.T.S. do this!!

– **Michael Nortune**, President of Open Bible Churches

Sean Dunn's magnum opus is a meticulously crafted work that deftly weaves theological profundity with heartfelt authenticity. This book is not merely a passive read but an invitation to engage deeply with the divine narrative of salvation, urging believers to become fervent ambassadors of reconciliation and grace. *Contending for the Rising Generations* is a tour de force that transcends mere inspiration, equipping its readers with a renewed sense of purpose. For anyone who treasures the eternal significance of leading others into the Kingdom, Sean's book is not just recommended; it is imperative.

- **Christian Thomas Lee**, Ministry Champion, Influencer

Sean Dunn is the leading voice on reaching the next generation. He has proven himself as an innovative thought leader and compassionate voice that gets mind-blowing results. This book is a beautiful representation of his expertise, passion, and effectiveness.

- **Gabrielle Bosché**, CEO, The Purpose Company

As the parents of three Gen Z children, my wife and I are keenly aware of the unique pressures this younger generation is facing. In addition, many families that we serve as wealth advisors are seeking wisdom on how to effectively engage this generation with the gospel. Drawing on decades of proven experience impacting Gen Z'ers and Millennials, in this timely book Sean Dunn accurately frames the current generational crisis, emphasizes the need for urgency in our response as Christ followers, and provides helpful direction for engaging the Gen Z/Millennial generations with God's message of hope and healing.

- **Brian Shepler**, CEO/President, Blue Trust

CONTENDING
for the Rising Generations

Winning Millennials and Gen Z with
the Hope of the Gospel

SEAN DUNN

BookJourney

Copyright © 2025 by Sean Dunn

BookJourney

Published by Book Journey Publishing | bookjourney.com
Book Journey Publishing, Castle Rock, Colorado, USA

ISBN 979-8-9911673-0-7
Library of Congress Control Number: 2025904511

All rights reserved. No part of this publication may be reproduced, stored in a retrieval system, or transmitted in any form or by any means—including photocopying, recording, or other electronic or mechanical methods—without the prior written permission of the publisher. The only exception is brief quotations in printed reviews.

All Scripture quotations, unless otherwise indicated, are taken from the Holy Bible, New International Version®, NIV®. Copyright ©1973, 1978, 1984, 2011 by Biblica, Inc.™ Used by permission of Zondervan. All rights reserved worldwide. The "NIV" and "New International Version" are trademarks registered in the United States Patent and Trademark Office by Biblica, Inc.™

Author's note: With the exception of my immediate family members, all names and identifying details have been changed to protect the confidentiality of my clients.

Cover and text design by Cynthia Young
Cover image © Gremlin/iStock

Contents

Dedication .... *ix*
Disclaimer .... *x*
Foreword .... *xi*

Introduction 1
Disconnected and Desperate 7
Dangerous Differences 21
What Message Are We Sending? 33
They Are Waiting 45
The Time Is Now 61
Earning the Right 75
Radical Assumptions 87
Purposeful Prompts 101
When They Walk Away 111
"Do I Matter?" 131
Fully Captured 147
The Power that Transforms 163
Time to Take Action 173

God's Rescue Plan *189*
Millennial and Gen Z Statistics *192*

Dedication

THIS BOOK is dedicated to the God of Heaven who sent His only begotten Son to rescue me from an eternity of suffering and separation.

To those who long to see the younger generations fully embrace Jesus Christ as their Lord and Savior.

To Jené, my amazing wife, who supports me and encourages me to pursue lost and hurting young people with the gospel message.

To those who are on mission with me as we Contend for the Rising Generations. Those who have prayed for me, rooted for me, served alongside of me, challenged me, and celebrated with me. This list includes those who have served on our board, ministry teams, as online volunteers, intercessors, staff, and those who have supported our mission financially.

Finally, this book is dedicated to those who do not yet know Jesus Christ and those who have not yet embraced His offer of grace and mercy. May you discover that He truly is good, He longs for a relationship with you, and He is the answer to every meaningful question you have.

Disclaimer

All names (besides my own and my wife, Jené) and specific identifying circumstances have been changed to protect the privacy of all individuals involved.

Foreword

THIS BOOK is not yet another interesting but dismissible treatment of an obscure subject, best relegated to a limited audience and parked on a virtual shelf. In fact, among the rest of the messages that will vie for your attention this year, *Contending for the Rising Generations* may be the most important challenge of all.

How is that distinction possible? As I've read Sean's passionate presentation of this material, its emphasis is clear: It call us into action to fight for our young people's eternity. Sean does not write as a theoretician, or a pulpit-pounder preaching to inflame but not inspire or lead the way. He and his Groundwire team have cracked the code of communication with the oncoming generations, Millennials and Gen Z who are too often closed to us.

Contemporary research, as organized and reported by George Barna, has exposed a tragic lack of clarity among church-attending Christians regarding their awareness of, and commitment to, the Great Commission. Barna's research found that only 51% of church-attending Christians knew the term "the Great Commission," and only one-third of those (17%) could cite it.

The Great Commission is most often cited as Jesus' last instructions to His apostles before returning to His Throne in Glory:

"All authority in Heaven and on Earth has been given to me. Therefore go and make disciples of all nations, baptizing them in the name of the Father and of the Son and of the Holy Spirit, and teaching them to obey everything I have commanded you. And surely I am with you always, to the very end of the age" (Matthew 28:18–20).

"It is not for you to know the times or dates the Father has set by his own authority. But you will receive power when the Holy Spirit comes on you; and you will be my witnesses in Jerusalem, and in all Judea and Samaria, and to the ends of the earth" (Acts 1:7–8).

Awareness is a start… but awareness alone doesn't ensure the assignment has been embraced as an active and successful pursuit. Is this just something that ministry leaders ponder, or does it represent a compelling directive to mainstream believers? Is the advancement of the Gospel message a delegated responsibility carried only by missionaries and ministers? Or is it the continuing agenda that should command the focus of all who call Him Lord?

The order to make disciples is the overarching mandate. The target communities—from the days of the Apostles to now—have always been "the others." Though Christianity started as an emergent movement within the First Century Jewish community, Jesus' gameplan was for His followers to break out of their close and comfortable relational circles to penetrate the difficult and distant communities who needed the gift of life. The Gospel was never intended to be restricted to those who were easily reached.

For 2000 years, missional expansion has been both geographic and ethnic. Crossing boundaries with Bibles has been the modus operandi for millennia, but those same cross-cultural challenges exist within our own nation and society. In America today, the separational distinction between generations mirrors the differences recognized between people groups internationally. Sean challenges us to recognize the isolation between the generations who currently share zip codes but lack connectivity. The spiritual insulation between Boomers, Busters, Millennials and Gen Zs is the Enemy's strategy to keep the flow of faith from happening between the aging churchgoers and the emerging church-avoiders. I've been watching God elevate Sean's leadership in reaching the tough crowd of apatheists (as Sean will introduce in Chapter 2) who are America's faith future.

Our intergenerational hand-off hangs in a precarious balance today. Will we mobilize a new wave of transformed followers of Jesus who will take our baton and lead revival in our land? Or will we miss the transfer because we didn't know—or learn—how to make the timeless Gospel timely?

The underlying foundation for every follower of Jesus should be a clear and compelling certainty of our Kingdom mission. In the language of modern society, we are to be in widespread agreement about the agenda for the faith community, *or in Bible-speak, "the church,"* regarding the Great Commission. It represents our principal engagement throughout the span of our lifetime. To use my friend Rick Warren's trademark phrase, the Great Commission is the most important challenge of living a Purpose-Driven life.

Cheri and I are avowed supporters of and advocates for the innovative mission that Sean and Jené lead with the Groundwire team. Their slim staff and expanding volunteers are creating breakthroughs for biblical faith that are defying human explanation. There is only one conclusion: God is at work and He is glorified.

Read with confidence that God may convict you toward action. That's where He's most known to create satisfying excitement in your spiritual journey!

— Bob Shank

Introduction

Since my youth, God, you have taught me, and to this day I declare your marvelous deeds. Even when I am old and gray, do not forsake me, my God, till I declare your power to the next generation, your mighty acts to all who are to come (Psalm 71:17–18).

IN TODAY's post-Christian culture, unchurched teens and young adults see Christianity as outdated and the church irrelevant. And they are suffering. The levels of anxiety, depression, and hopelessness among youth in our nation have never been higher. Somehow, the emerging generations have lost sight of the absolutes of life, causing them to struggle with their identity and a lack of purpose. They have veered away from God's truth.

The Enemy has declared war over our nation's young. It is time for us to rise up and contend for them, connect with them on a personal level with authenticity and love, win them back. It's up to us to help point them to Jesus, the source of purpose and joy these very young people are craving.

You might be a parent or a grandparent of a Millennial or Gen Z who has walked away from the faith you raised them in. Or you might be a concerned leader working with confused, hurting youth. Perhaps God has been stirring your heart with a burden for certain teens or young adults in your life, whether a neighbor, a server at your favorite restaurant, or the kid who mows your lawn. Whatever your role in the lives of young people, I am glad you are here. The need is great.

After ministering to teens and young adults for nearly four decades, I'm seeing a noticeable shift with today's youth. They are more open to the gospel of Jesus than you might think. They just don't know how to connect with the eternal hope Jesus offers. That is the purpose of this book. In *Contending for the Rising Generations,* I will show you how, together, we can capture a generation with the love of Jesus. We must. God is calling our generation to contend for the ones who follow.

Captured with a Calling

It started out as a typical Sunday night service at church. The goal of the night was horizontal, and I settled in with forty of my best friends as we elbowed each other, cracked jokes, and were being just plain disruptive.

Until something changed.

Somewhere between the first song and the closing prayer, I became captured with God's presence and I couldn't move. Before I knew what had happened, all my friends had left, and I was the only one remaining. I don't remember what the preacher said that night. I don't remember the topic or what Scriptures we examined. All I knew was God had arrested my attention.

I was only fourteen, but that night I had a life-defining moment with the Lord. He called me to a life of passionate pursuit of Himself. I was already a believer, but I wasn't pursuing Him fully. At the same time, I also felt God placing a calling on my life. As clearly as if He and I were having a sit-down conversation, I heard Him calling me to a passionate pursuit of young people.

He dropped a phrase into my heart that has stayed with me to this day. His marching orders were so clear that I actually wrote what I heard in the back of my blue King James Bible: "Contend for a generation." In that moment, I was called to a lifetime of fighting for, contending for, pursuing youth and young adults for an eternity with Jesus.

Having a mission statement as a teenager makes you a bit odd, and I was. Although I did some of the things that a typical young male did—chase girls and over prioritize sports—my focus became sharing my faith and pursuing other teens for Christ. I was not perfect, just ask my parents, but I knew I was called to youth ministry. At eighteen years of age, I was hired to serve as the youth leader in charge of a local church's youth ministry, and I have been contending for the younger generations ever since.

Over the decades, I have served in local churches, traveled full time as a speaker, and written several books (the last one in 2008). As Founder and President of Groundwire Ministries since 1995,

I continue to pursue young people who don't know Jesus in the same personal and loving way that I do. Since you're reading this, I'm pretty sure you know Jesus intimately as well, but too many in the emerging generations have either lost sight of who Jesus is or have never seen Him clearly. Because of this, they don't understand what He sees when He looks at them and all that He offers them.

As I approach forty years in vocational youth ministry, my passion for Jesus continues to drive me, as does my calling to connect the younger generations with the God who loves them and wants to save them. I pray this is also your passion and that together we can continue to hear God's voice leading as we lean into the opportunity to connect a generation to the goodness of God.

In the coming pages, I will share insight from my experience, from volunteers with Groundwire, and from the invaluable stories from Millennials and Gen X themselves.

One interesting note here—I do believe I am more effective now in reaching and contending for young people than I have ever been, as I have learned more about my audience and discovered how to most effectively approach them with the story and purpose of Jesus. It has become a priority for me and the Groundwire team to understand the young people we are trying to reach. Teens and young adults are different from when I was growing up, and today's culture is significantly different than it was even ten years ago. Just look at the shift in spiritual beliefs and moral values in our society since you and I were their age. Some would say young people are harder to reach than ever before, but I believe certain transitions in our world, and in their lives, have made them easier to reach. Some of their struggles make God's offer of hope, peace, and love even more attractive to them. I can't wait to share with you many of the learnings that give me hope as, together, we focus on contending for the emerging generations.

They look different—but there is hope.

One of the tools I use to assist audiences of adults—pastors, business leaders, parents, and grandparents—understand the young people in their lives is a Generation Quiz. The quiz is interactive and eye-opening. Its purpose is to help concerned adults realize the cultural shifts and spiritual differences between them and the ones they pray for, love, and long to reach.

Recently, after walking a crowd through the quiz and highlighting the challenges the younger generations face and the beliefs they have embraced, a businessman who was also a father approached me. What he said caught me off guard.

"Sean, at first I loved the quiz… until I didn't."

He went on to tell me that the data startled him and made him sad. He didn't realize how desperate and hopeless the young people were.

After a short conversation, he did end with, "But my sadness is gone. After the rest of your talk, I am encouraged and excited. It gave me hope when you shared how open they are to Jesus and how many are coming to faith."

He left with his eyes opened to the realities of the younger generations as well as prepared and encouraged with hope to reach them with God's truth.

I bring up that conversation because some of the data shared in the initial chapters of this book might leave you feeling sad or handcuffed. Don't give up; the good news is coming. In *Contending for the Rising Generations,* you will better understand those you care about. You will be given tools that will help you pray for them aggressively and have meaningful spiritual conversations with them.

As we walk through this book and the challenge of contending for the rising generations together, my hope is that you will be reminded that:

God is still good,

The gospel is still powerful,

And the harvest is still ripe.

CHAPTER 1

Disconnected and Desperate

In your righteousness, rescue me and deliver me; turn your ear to me and save me (Psalm 71:2).

How do you reach a young person who is completely isolated and overwhelmed? How do you get the message of Jesus to the college student who is drowning in pain and wallowing in misery? What about the single mom who is devastated because of a broken relationship and failing to keep positive perspectives? And how do we reach a youth who has bought into the lies of today's culture and is living their "own truth"?

You know the type of young person I am talking about. You see them every day. Perhaps in your neighborhood. Maybe even around your table. They are desperate for help and hope, but they will not pursue spiritual voices and they behave as if they are not open to a conversation about the God of hope.

Our hearts break for them, for we see in them their struggle. We worry and pray, but we can't seem to find the chink in their armor that allows us access to encourage, inspire, and interject Jesus. We don't know how to capture their attention effectively in a way that sheds the light of Jesus into their darkness.

That is the purpose of this book. I want to share with you what we have learned at Groundwire and what is working every day as we reach out to the lost and hurting young people all around the nation.

In order to get us pointed in the right direction, let me start by sharing a true story that represents the desperation and willingness of the younger generations.

A young woman named Megan sat alone in her bedroom, hopelessness overwhelming her. As she scrolled mindlessly on her phone, she contemplated how to ease her misery. Just then, a Groundwire commercial popped up. The ad on her mobile screen showed the words "When life hurts, Jesus cares," followed by an invitation to chat with someone. With nothing to lose, the girl logged in.

An older woman named Anne responded to the chat from her home in California. Megan, who was 19 years old, admitted she was struggling to not harm herself. She explained she'd been cutting herself for years. Anne assured the young woman Jesus wants to help her and that He's only a prayer away, but Megan felt too broken. She told Anne she had lost her faith.

"What happened that you lost your faith?" Anne asked.

"I tried to kill myself."

Megan went on to explain how a Christian, someone Megan thought she could trust, condemned her for her suicide attempt and accused her of being attention-seeking. The friend blamed Megan for all the bad things happening to her.

"It hurt a lot," Megan admitted.

"I'm sure it did. Hurtful words cut the heart." Anne opened up to the broken girl, sharing her own story of brokenness. She identified with Megan, assuring her she understood her hurt. Then Anne told her how much Jesus wants to heal her pain and give her peace.

The online conversation continued as Anne prayed for Megan, showed her hope, and eventually led the young woman in prayer to accept Jesus. After the prayer, Megan made a confession.

"Can I tell you something? I came on here as a last resort. I have 168 tablets I was going to take to end my life. Now I'm going to flush them down the toilet."

Anne waited online as Megan flushed the pills away. Within a few moments, Megan returned with, "Done!" The two women talked some more and eventually Megan threw the blade away as well as Anne waited again. They exchanged emails and prayed together before the online chat finally ended.

We see hopeless desperation and the need for hope, just like Megan's, every day at Groundwire. Believe me, there is an urgency to reach the younger generations, and we must learn how to reach them where they are. Not with condemnation like Megan's "friend," but with the unconditional love of Jesus that Anne showed.

I wish you could experience the conversations with these young people through our ministry at Groundwire. Over and over, we hear stories that reflect a despair that comes from a lack of purpose. Like the teen who grew up with an abusive, alcoholic dad and feels worthless with no future plans in sight, or the girl who searches for acceptance from boys but is used and abandoned, or the young people who struggle with their own identity, losing sight of what is real and what is not. Every day, the younger generations are dealing with fear and panic, loneliness, suicidal ideation, identity confusion, a desperation that screams for answers they can trust. The younger generations are in trouble.

So, who do I mean when I say younger generations? Let me explain.

Explaining the Generations

I'd be willing to guess that since you're reading this book, you are part of the Baby Boomer generation. Or perhaps you're a bit younger—from Generation X. Baby Boomers were born between 1946 and 1964. Gen X started arriving on the scene in 1965 until 1980 or so. Baby Boomers and Gen X would be considered the older generations. Sorry, my Gen X friends. We have officially hit middle age.

Our "younger generations" include Generation Y, or most commonly referred to as Millennials. Millennials were born between 1981 and 1996, followed by Gen Z, born 1997–2010. According to Brittanica.com,[1] Generation Alpha is the working name for the newest generation of Americans who are still being born (2010-2025). Since most Generation Alpha children have

---

1. Eldridge, Stephen, Generation Alpha Demographic Group, Brittanica, (2023). https://www.britannica.com/topic/Generation-Alpha

Millennial parents, they are sometimes called "mini-Millennials." This book focuses on how to reach the Millennials and Gen Z.

What we continually see through our ministry at Groundwire is that the younger generations are growing up apart from a healthy relationship with Christ. Of course, this doesn't include the faithful few who are living in the faith of their parents, or in their own faith. But the majority of Millennials and Gen Z do not have a personal relationship with Jesus. According to recent studies, while nearly half of Gen Z individuals report having made a commitment to Jesus, only a small percentage (around 13%) are considered "biblically engaged,"[2] meaning they regularly interact with Scripture and have a deep understanding of Jesus' teachings; this indicates that while many Gen Z individuals may identify as Christian, a significantly smaller portion have a strong personal relationship with Jesus based on active Bible study.

This disconnect affects everything in their sphere—their identity, their anxiety, their fear. It affects their morality and impacts their relationships. Their separation from God impacts basically everything that's going on in their world. They have no moral compass, no biblical worldview. They are chasing their tails, trying to find purpose and joy and peace and love and all the things we long for as human beings. And they don't know where to find the answers. They are directionless, leaderless, stuck in patterns of misery.

2. Fulks, J., Petersen, R., & Plake, J. F. (2022). State of the Bible 2022. American Bible Society

And this misery is creating a destructive cycle. The American Psychological Association states one in three young people in Generation Z struggles with anxiety, depression, or other mental health challenges, and suicide rates have drastically risen.[3] Other studies show 46% of Gen Z feel anxious or stressed "most of" or "all of" the time.[4] Not just once in a while. Nearly half of our young people feel anxious or depressed the majority of the time. No wonder suicidal ideation has become such a widespread problem in these age groups. Other destructive symptoms threaten our kids as well, like substance abuse, eating disorders, sexual and gender confusion, and so many more. These are major issues.

Social media plays into these toxic issues as well, especially with the onslaught of Instagram, TikTok, and new platforms constantly popping up. Kids are endlessly dealing with the challenges of comparison. They see their friends' posts online, causing them to compare their worst days with other people's best, and they think *I'm the only one who's not living my dream. I'm the only one who isn't taking these great vacations, eating these great meals, going on these great dates.* And they feel left out because friends are hanging out while they're sitting at home alone.

3. American Psychological Association, Stress in America™. (2020). https://www.apa.org/news/press/releases/stress/2020/report-october/
4. Mental health today. A deep dive based on the 2023 Gen Z and Millennial survey. Deloitte. (2023, May). https://www2.deloitte.com/content/dam/Deloitte/global/Documents/deloitte-2023-genz-millennial-survey-mental-health.pdf

They feel like they're the only person who's not living their best life. Which is in and of itself a lie. Our next generation kids are entrenched in the mindset of YOLO: you only live once. That's not true. You only live forever. But young people are living for the moment. They don't prioritize the future, much less eternity.

> YOLO stands for You Only Live Once. That's not true—you only live forever.

There has always been a lingering misery and struggle and depression among young people. Most older adults will agree that the years entering into adulthood are not easy. Teens and young adults struggle to find themselves and adapt to all the changes as they approach independence. Social media has shifted the dynamics even further. A study of eighth, tenth, and twelfth graders from 1991 to 2023 asked quality-of-life questions such as, *"Are you happy?" "Do you find purpose in life?"* Eighteen percent of them answered negatively in 1991. The climb was gradual until they spiked right around 2010 when social media became more prevalent. The numbers spiked again in 2020 when the COVID pandemic increased isolation and exacerbated our kids' unhappiness even more. By 2023, statistics from the quality-of-life questions reveal young people answered negatively between 48%–52% of the time.[5]

5. Twenge, Jean. (2023) "Monitoring the Future: Depressive Symptoms in US 8th, 10th, and 12th Graders"

More than unhappy, our kids are desperate. They crave purpose, joy, peace, hope, love, forgiveness, direction. Ultimately salvation. But they're looking in the wrong places. The number one place Gen Z goes when feeling anxious or stressed is TikTok.[6] They're longing for healthy relationships, and they're struggling to find joy and happiness wherever they can find it. They don't know who they are, so they're just striving for *something*. It's as if they're trapped in water and the more they tread, the more they lose the ability to keep themselves up. They search for something to hold on to that will give them stability, but they gravitate toward things that quickly sink, taking a portion of their identity and quality-of-life with them.

This isn't about addressing the symptoms.
It's about getting to the core.

The younger generations are living isolated lives, not walking with their Creator; therefore, they don't know why they were created and they don't know the power of the Creator in their life. So they keep trying to do it on their own. The destructive symptoms are pulling them farther and deeper into the water, and they don't even realize it. They are broken and worn down, weary and burdened.

6. Garnham, C. (2022, September 1). The Gen Z Mental Health save-what is causing the surge?. HealthMatch. https://healthmatch.io/blog/the-gen-z-mental-health-wave-what-is-causing-the-surge

My calling, as well as that of parents, grandparents, leaders, friends, is not about addressing the symptoms. It's about getting to the core. Millennials and Gen Z might not know what to ask for. But what they really need is Jesus. He is the One who answers every meaningful question and meets every significant need. Jesus calls to every single one of these young people, *Come to me, all you who are weary and burdened, and I will give you rest* (Matthew 11:28). And they need our help to find Him.

One Life

One of my staff members recommended I watch a movie named *One Life*.[7] Released in 2023, the film is based on the true story of Nicholas (Nicky) Winton, a broker in London who rescued hundreds of mostly Jewish children at the onset of WWII.

In December 1938, Nicky learned of the impending invasion of Nazis into his ancestral homeland of Czechoslovakia. He rode the train from London to Prague and was heartbroken at what he saw. Thousands of refugees, families and children, who had already fled Germany and Austria because of Nazi occupation, were living in pitiful conditions within the impoverished city. Their make-shift structures could hardly be called shelter, and they had very little food. Many were dying of starvation and winter had just begun. Nicky observed hordes of children, some with families and many

---

7. "One Life" directed by James Hawes (2023; released in the United Kingdom on January 1, 2024 and in the United States on March 15, 2024), See-Saw Films, MBK Productions, and BBC Film.

with no parents or guardians, living in the mud with little hope of surviving the winter, much less the Nazi invasion. He knew something needed to be done.

The movie shows Nicky trying to convince a small group of his friends and colleagues to help him rescue the children. The daunting task seems impossible. They would need to find individual foster homes in London for every single child, coordinate the transport of large groups of children via the train, obtain overwhelming pages of documentation from government officials who had other things on their mind besides relocating children. It would take an army of people cooperating with one another to make it happen, all under the threat of a Nazi invasion any day. In the movie during this discussion, one of Nicky's friends asks him why he believes saving the children is their responsibility.

Nicky replies, "I have seen it and I can't unsee it. I can do something, therefore I must."

A colleague says, "You have a lot of faith in ordinary people."

"I have to, I am one."

One of the other men agrees. "Me too."

Nicky's response resonated with me. "This is what we need, an army of ordinaries."

In a race against the threatening invasion, Nicky spearheaded a massive plan that in the end rescued 669 children from the Nazis. When I heard the number of children he'd saved, I cheered. But Nicky Winton was regretful his entire life for the ones he was unable to rescue. The Nazis invaded Prague in March 1939, trapping and eventually killing most of the remaining Jewish families and children.

I won't give away the rest of the story, only encourage you to see the movie. Nicky Winton and his army of ordinaries not only rescued hundreds of children; they shifted the course of countless families forever.

In today's culture, we are facing the impending takeover of the Enemy. He is in fierce pursuit of our next generations. In *One Life*, Nicky's heart broke at the sight of kids living in the mud, alone, starving, cold, in danger. Many of the children had no parents. Some were carrying the weight of responsibilities too heavy for their age. One 12-year-old girl had taken on the responsibility of caring for an abandoned infant. No one knew what happened to the baby's parents. Kids were taking care of kids without the guidance of the very adults who should be protecting them. In our world today, our kids are sitting in the mud of social media and the filth of ungodly beliefs. They are consumed by cultural attitudes that threaten their identity and their lives, their eternity. They need an army of ordinaries who are prayerful, compassionate, motivated, and determined to rescue them from the Enemy. To show them the hope Jesus offers.

Like Nicky's valiant team, we are also in a race against time. Millions of our lost young people are trapped, unable to get out from behind Enemy lines on their own, and he is hellbent on destroying them. Megan would have been lost to the Enemy if she hadn't connected with Anne online. Anne is one of the ordinaries who, like Nicky, sees the mud our kids are living in. She has seen it and she can't unsee it. She believes she can do something, so she does. This Baby Boomer chooses to fight for the younger generations, rescuing one life at a time, simply by making herself available to talk with hurting young people about Jesus.

Real People

One hot summer day, grandparents Gilda and Jorge took their grandkids for a day of fun at Six Flags. The sun rose and heated up quickly as the extended family worked their way through tangled crowds and long lines. They had to talk loudly to hear one another above the blaring music, not to mention the piercing screams from riders thundering by on noisy rides. For a quick moment of rest, Gilda and her husband, Jorge, sat in the shade and watched passersby as they waited for their grandkids to finish a ride. Suddenly, without saying a word, the couple turned to one another with troubled looks on their faces. They'd been looking in different directions, but they both saw the same thing: lost young people who were lonely, hurting, broken. These weren't smiling, happy kids spending an innocent day at an amusement park. These were young people who were begging to be noticed, because social invisibility is something they could not handle. Their edgy clothes and over-the-top behavior of acting out revealed how much they were craving attention. Many were awkward and outcasts, and they knew it. They were aimless, wandering, lost.

This older couple's perspective switched in that moment. They stopped seeing the busyness and the chaos and the crazy crowd and started seeing real people. Real people who need Jesus.

Gilda is the leader of our Spanish ministry at Groundwire. At our next team prayer time, she shared the Six Flags experience, and we prayed fervently as a team, again, for the millions of hurting people in the younger generations. Young people who will do one of two things through eternity. They will either celebrate through eternity, or they will suffer through it.

> People will do one of two things through eternity: They will either celebrate through eternity, or they will suffer through it.

Our young people are suffering, and they're not sure why. They are so consumed with the misery of their lives that they have no room in their minds to think about eternity. It's not even on their radar. The next generations aren't waking up and saying, *"I am going to hell."* They are waking up and saying, *"I am going through hell."* For them, an eternity of suffering has already begun. Their constant, daily suffering and struggle prevents them from thinking beyond today, at what lies ahead of them eternally.

We will either celebrate through eternity with Jesus or we will suffer through it without Him. Those are the only two options for any of us. That's why it is so important we learn how to understand the Millennials and Gen Z. We must learn how to share

Jesus with them so they won't stay trapped behind Enemy lines, suffering through eternity.

Some readers will pick up this book because they want to understand their children or grandchildren. They might not be thinking about much more than trying to figure out what's going on in today's culture. I understand that. Today's culture continues to shift in and out of all kinds of confusion. It's a struggle for any of us to understand. But the struggle is bigger than what we face today. It's critical we think about eternity—in light of ourselves as well as our children. And here is the good news. Keeping this perspective of eternity will empower us to influence and impact—rescue—our kids and grandkids, as well as other trapped young people we meet.

The spiritual future of all the younger generations lies on the hinges of what happens today. You and I, the older generations, can lead the way for the emerging generations to choose Jesus, to celebrate with Him through eternity. We must contend for a generation as if lives depend on it, because they do.

In the pages ahead, I will provide you with tools to not only better understand the young people in your life but also strategies to help you pray for them, encourage them, have conversations with them, and intentionally introduce them to Jesus. Together, our army of ordinaries can rescue the next generations from an eternity of suffering.

CHAPTER 2

Dangerous Differences

I will search for the lost and bring back the strays. I will bind up the injured and strengthen the weak (Ezekiel 34:16a).

THE GENERATIONS of today are not the same as the generations of yesterday. They are different in so many ways, and it's imperative we recognize those differences. Kids believe and value different "truths" than the older generations do. Even the message of Jesus, and the real truth of who He is, is being twisted in today's culture. As churchgoers, the majority of us know who the real Jesus is. We are familiar with the Bible and God's plan of salvation. But too often, we don't understand our audience—Millennials and Gen Z—and therefore we're not connecting with them. We also don't know where they are because we don't hang out where they do. To contend for the younger generations, we need to know our audience and we need to know where to find them.

Know Our Audience

It will probably come as no surprise when I say, for the most part, Baby Boomers and many Gen X don't comprehend the differences between themselves and the younger generations. We tend to think they're just like us, that they believe the same things we do and share the same values. *Of course, they value what we value,* we think. Why wouldn't they? I met with a guy recently who values church, and he doesn't understand why young people don't value church. Well, they don't.

> To contend for the younger generations, we need to know our audience and we need to know where to find them.

When desiring to impact young lives, we must understand our priorities are different from theirs. We need to only look around to see many Millennial and Gen Z couples living together without a marriage certificate, a sharp contrast from older generations who view marriage and family as core life goals. When talking about worldview, Boomers matured amid a culture that embraced a biblical worldview, while that started to decline with Gen X and the decline is escalating. Today, 10% of Millennials have a biblical worldview compared to only 4% of Gen Z.[8] And a non-biblical worldview opens the door to adopting beliefs outside of God's design. Gen Z has the highest percentage of any generation, with one in five identifying as LGBTQ, reflecting a major shift

---

8. Morrow, Jonathan. (2024). Only 4 Percent of Gen Z Have a Biblical Worldview. https://www.impact360institute.org/articles/4-percent-gen-z-biblical-worldview/

in how the younger generations perceive identity and sexuality.[9]

The older generations tend to focus on morality or culture or church attendance. Millennials and Gen Z crave hope, purpose, peace, joy, connection. Their values aren't in line with the older generations' values. So when we try to connect with them about matters of faith, the message is off.

We older adults often come at kids from the perspective of a didactic approach, striving to teach them what we're convinced they should know or enlighten them on how they should behave. There are some who like to share their knowledge and their opinions to make sure everyone is in agreement. That's not what the next generations need. It is not what they respond to. Young people, first and foremost, need Jesus.

We must understand that a 19-year-old today is very different from a 19-year-old in the older generations. If you rewind to when Baby Boomers were ages 17 to 25, it was easier to capture their spiritual attention. During those years, Christianity was more mainstream than it is now. Regular church attendance and belief in Jesus were the societal norm. And for those right behind the Boomers… Gen X, well… they were easier to entertain. Throughout the 1980s and '90s, churches held special events, movie nights, and weekly youth groups with games, and then slipped the message of Jesus in.

9. Jones, Jeffery M. (2024) "LGBT Identification in U.S. Ticks up to 7.1%" https://news.gallup.com/poll/389792/lgbt-identification-ticks-up.aspx/

Today a 17- or 19-year-old is feeling more overwhelmed. Kids today are being bombarded from every direction. Young people are witnessing school shootings, watching their friends die by suicide, dealing with bullies, constantly receiving ungodly messages from a messed up culture—and they're struggling to cope with it all. Statistics show 90% of substance use disorders (SUDs) start during the teenage years.[10] Millennials and Gen Z feel like a proverbial cloud follows them. The younger generations are definitely more willing to talk about their brokenness and struggles, but they're not going to the right place for help.

We must understand that a 19-year-old today is very different than a 19-year-old in the older generations.

As young people, when Boomers and Gen X went through difficult times, we sought help from trusted adults. We went to therapists, teachers, coaches, pastors, and parents for advice. The younger generations have this mentality of *I have to do it on my own*. So what do they do when they have had a bad day? The next generations go online. They go to TikTok,[11] they vent on

---

10. Gomez, S. (2024, April 15). Gen Z and Addiction. Addiction Center. https://www.addictioncenter.com/addiction/gen-z-addiction/
11. Garnham, C. (2022, September 1). The Gen Z Mental Health save-what is causing the surge?. HealthMatch. https://healthmatch.io/blog/the-gen-z-mental-health-wave-what-is-causing-the-surge

socials with peers who "get it," or they binge on Hulu, YouTube, or video games.

Or they take on an altruistic angle, concerned about how to fix all the injustices in our society. Research shows Gen Z is incredibly justice oriented. Nearly one-third of Gen Z (32%) are regularly engaged in activism or social justice work (compared to 24% of Millennials), demonstrating a significant Gen Z commitment to societal change. This engagement deepens among college students, where the percentage escalates to nearly 40%. In the realm of public demonstrations, over half of Gen Z (51%) have participated in rallies or protests to support specific causes or social issues, with a slight increase to 56% observed among those in higher ed.[12] Most young people talk about seeking social justice, but I don't think social justice is really their goal—it may be who they want to be, intellectual and purpose driven, but in reality they are trapped by and led by their emotions. Especially their negative and overwhelming emotions—and they are consumed by perceptions of self. Their goal is to make sure they get through their day, which can feel like an impossible challenge some days. What they're actually seeking is survival.

And because they're working hard to survive, they're not seeking spiritual things. We've all heard the phrase "seeker sensitive"—as in seeker-sensitive churches and ministry models. The younger generations aren't seeking, whereas the older generations did. Our

12. United Way of the National Capital Area. (2024, March 5) Blog: "The Gen Z Activism Survey". https://unitedwaynca.org/blog/gen-z-activism-survey/

young people hold an entirely different view on spirituality than we did at their age. Not only are they not as spiritually curious, Millennials and Gen Z are also steering further away from God's plumb line of truth. When asked about moral truth, 83% believe moral truth depends on your circumstances. Only 6% said moral truth is absolute.[13]

During the time of Baby Boomers and Gen X growing up, there were Christians who believed in the God of the Bible, and there were atheists who denied His existence. Then we had this middle group many people called agnostic. The agnostic of the older generations wasn't committed either way—to believing in God or not believing in Him—yet they seemed to retain some curiosity. They reflected the mentality of *"I don't know what I believe, but I've got to figure it out."*

In today's culture, 7% of Millennials and 13% of Gen Z are atheists. Atheists do not believe in God. For Gen Z, atheist is no longer a dirty word: The percentage of teens who identify as such is double that of the general population (13% vs. 6% of all adults). The proportion that identifies as Christian likewise drops from generation to generation.[14] Then on the other side

---

13. Barna Group. (n.d.). Americans Are Most Likely to Base Truth on Feelings. Barna. https://www.barna.com/research/americans-are-most-likely-to-base-truth-on-feelings/

14. Atheism doubles among generation Z. Barna Group. (2023, August 16). https://www.barna.com/research/atheism-doubles-among-generation-z/

of the spectrum are the comparatively few who love Jesus. This percentage of young people love church. It's where they find their identity, it's where they find their hope, it's where they find their tribe. These kids need our support and our prayers. They are a minority in an increasingly worldly culture.

So we still have atheists and Christians, but now we have a new third category for the majority of Gen Z. These kids fall in the category of what the Urban Dictionary calls the apatheist. I first heard about this up-and-coming word in 2021. At that time the definition read: *"A young person who believes in God but ignores him."* That pretty much describes the mentality of countless young people in our world today.

Apatheist is basically a woke word for agnostic. Consider this category as "apathy" with "ist" on the end. They just don't care. So they're not saying like the agnostics of the older generations, *"I don't know what I believe, but I've got to figure it out."* They're saying, *"I don't know what I believe. Period. And I'm okay with that."* Spiritual belief is just not a priority for Millennials or Gen Z.

Unlike an atheist who adamantly denies God's existence, an apatheist typically believes in God. But they're not asking any questions about Him or making any attempt to know Him. You don't hear an apatheist asking, *"If I believed in God, my next question would be: What does that mean to me? How does that impact me? How should that affect me?"* Instead, they say, *"Yeah, I believe in God. Or I don't. So what?"* and they go on to other things in their life. Even when they believe in God, they ignore Him; He doesn't really matter much to them.

Some young people who are apatheists actually claim to be atheists, but that's rarely the truth. They spout the term "post-theism" as a defense to not have to believe in a higher being. They try to claim that belief in God is obsolete, that only "less developed" humans still believe in such an "outdated concept." This is what they want to believe, because if God is real, then there would be a need for accountability, and they don't want that. So they cling to the idea, *"There is no God."* But from what I experience day in and day out as I engage young people in conversation, is that they don't truly accept that; they just don't care enough to search for the truth. They're not sitting in their rooms at night asking if God is real, if He loves them, if He is good, if He sees them.

When Baby Boomers and Gen X were 15- to 25-years-old, there was a little more desire in us to get those questions answered. Millennials and Gen Z are not asking spiritual questions. When it comes to God and spirituality, the younger generations are often disinterested, and they are drifting more and more away from God's truth and love. They need us more than ever to learn how to reach them with the life-giving message of Jesus.

In the Way

Yet, here is a sad truth I've seen over and over. Even if today's young people were spiritually curious and were asking questions about God and eternity, Christians have the tendency to get in the way. This has got to change, and that requires looking at ourselves and our attitudes honestly.

Back when I worked with teens at a local church, a new girl walked in as we were starting our youth group meeting. One of the regular attendees grunted and said, "Ugh. I can't believe *Jennifer* is here. She's the biggest slut in school."

"Why aren't you being kind to her?" I asked, somewhat surprised at her negative reaction.

"Oh, she has a horrible reputation."

"Well, I'm glad she's here. I'm grateful she somehow got up the courage to walk into a church. She needs to be met with compassion, not with judgment. She already feels judged."

Jennifer came from a broken home and had a terrible family life. Word around town is that one of her parents was in prison and that she was loose and easy, making everything even more difficult for her.

I added, "You know what really makes me sad? It's that Jennifer will never meet Christ if Christians keep getting in the way." Somebody who desperately needed what Jesus offers was being rejected by the people who claim to know and love and obey Jesus because they didn't want to be "infected" or "soiled."

Amazingly, Jennifer ended up sticking around and three weeks later she surrendered her life to Christ. And thankfully, one of the girls in our youth group ended up befriending Jennifer and came alongside her in her newfound faith.

Know Where They Are

Jennifer walked into our church 30 years ago. That rarely happens today. Let's begin with where they are not: Millennials and Gen Z are not attending church. Now, I want to take just a moment to highlight the benefit of the local church and the impact it has had on me and on so many young people in previous generations. I am not suggesting we defund the youth ministry model. I am simply implying that although the traditional youth ministry model is effective for a portion of the younger generations, the majority—the ones we want to focus on reaching (those who are desperate, hopeless, and lost)—will not show up on Sunday morning or Wednesday night. Game nights and all-night sleepovers at the church won't attract new outsiders like they used to. These tactics work for some, but not for the majority. You won't find the majority of the next generations at Christian youth rallies or conferences. These events are occupied by kids who are already a part of the church, which is great, but not many curious visitors are interested in Christian or church activities these days.

The one place where you can find Millennials and Gen Z hanging out for hours every day is staring at their phones. They're online. They're texting, scrolling. Their attention is grabbed by the latest in fashion, music, movies, tips and tricks, gossip, as it all speeds by in front of them for hours. And when I say hours, I mean *hours*. ABC News reported kids are on their phones an average of 7 hours and 22 minutes a day.[15] The average Gen Z has 8.5 social media accounts in their name.[16] This is the main reason Groundwire targets ads for mobile devices. We know that's where they are. We see this as a great opportunity. We know more than ever before how to capture a kid's attention through their phone. A church in a community might have access to 20% of the populace if it's a very significant, very, very unique church. Groundwire can get to 98% of young people right through that small device in their hands.

Millennials and Gen Z spend more time in front of a mobile screen than we ever could have imagined when we were their age. But kids are also in our homes, down the street, at the coffee shop, hanging out at the mall, the neighborhood park; some are at Six Flags. They're not inside our churches, but they're not far away, and they always have their phones with them. The younger generations aren't necessarily in a place where they're hearing the message of Jesus. That means we need to take it to them. All we need to do is ask God to lead us in their direction.

15. Jacobo, J. (2019, October 29). Teens spend more than 7 hours on screens for entertainment a day: Report. ABC News. https://abcnews.go.com/US/teens-spend-hours-screens-entertainment-day-report/story?id=66607555

16. Kakadia, K. (2023, March 30). A comprehensive list of social media statistics for journalists. Sociallyin Insider. https://blog.sociallyin.com/social-media-statistics-for-journalists-by-sociallyin

CHAPTER 3

What Message Are We Sending?

For I resolved to know nothing while I was with you except Jesus Christ and him crucified (1 Corinthians 2:2).

ONCE WAS in a restaurant for a meeting with a gentleman I did not know well. When the server walked up, I struck up a conversation. She told us about her teen son who was in trouble. She suspected he might even be in a gang. When I offered to pray for her son, she got down on her knees, folded her hands, and put her elbows on our table.

She closed her eyes really tight and immediately I had two thoughts: 1) *She hasn't prayed since she was three,* and 2) *She is desperate for help.*

After we prayed and she got up, I told her she didn't have to do this alone. I started to interject Jesus into the conversation, and she was leaning in, hungry to hear more. Just then, the guy I was with interrupted me and started telling this hurting mom that if she wants her son to make good decisions, it's about time she started making good decisions herself. He told her to go to church and take her kid with her. She couldn't leave our table fast enough.

33

This sad story is the perfect picture of the difference between Jesus and religion. At Jesus and everything He offered, she was open, interested, leaning in. When religion came up, the control, the *"Hey, you are broken"* judgment and the *"You've done this wrong"* condemnation, she ran in the other direction.

I've seen this time and time again. Christians are getting in the way because they lead with the wrong message. Teens and young adults are turned away from Jesus because Christians focus on their behavior instead of on the hope and healing that comes from a relationship with Jesus.

Even when we think our focus is on Jesus, the message we too often convey isn't the message that is heard. And it's having damaging effects. As the older generation, we continually send a message to the younger generations, whether we realize it or not. It is imperative we recognize the message we're sharing.

> It is imperative we recognize the message we're sharing.

In our hearts, as followers of Jesus, we want to be sharing the message of His truth and love, but as imperfect human beings, we sometimes communicate the opposite. Instead of pointing kids toward Jesus, if we're not walking in a personal, daily, surrendered relationship with Him, the message we're living can threaten to turn them away. The message we should be communicating is a passion to connect a generation to Christ, helping them understand how much they are loved, and how Jesus answers everything. But that's not always what they see. Sadly, we have unintentionally placed roadblocks in their way.

Roadblocks and Obstacles

I doubt any of us have done this on purpose, but the truth remains. We older generations have created obstacles that turn younger generations away from the very place where they could receive the answers.

ROADBLOCK & OBSTACLE 1: THEY DON'T SEE LOVE

The love that Jesus shows us and that He so clearly lived while He was on Earth speaks a message of unconditional, one-person-at-a-time love. Sadly, we don't represent Him well. Many Christians have a bad reputation of being known as close-minded, self-absorbed, and grumpy. Our young people don't understand the victory and the freedom that comes in surrendering to Jesus because it hasn't been modeled for them. Our lives don't reflect joy or compassion, so it's no wonder the next generations aren't attracted to what we believe.

Millennials and Gen Z also see Christians, the regular church-going kind, as judgmental. Why is that? What are we doing to cast this message? Perhaps our looks of disapproval at a group of young people in immodest dress? Our scowls at their music? Pious comments posted on our social media pages condemning today's culture definitely don't help. That might be one of the reason

Millennials and Gen Z have migrated away from Facebook.

As the older, hopefully wiser, generation, it's time we ask ourselves some tough questions. What makes us comfortable? Do we prefer the peaceful day-to-day within our churches? Do we anticipate growing "our" church with "holy and upright" people just like us instead of pursuing edgy young people from outside of our comfort zone? I want to challenge each of us to take a close look at what matters most and shift our priority from *"what would help those young people shape up"* to *"how can I most effectively communicate the love of Christ to that person?"*

And let's be honest. We can get so busy recruiting for the local church that we stop being the church and representing Jesus. We're so busy with church activities that we too often don't take the time to allow the love of God to renew our spirit—leaving us dry and unloving toward others (more on this later). Our misguided focus is too often on comfort and stability within our Christian community, rather than messing it up with the messes of a lost generation.

When all kids see is disapproval, they don't see the love of Christ coming through. Oh, we'll say we love others. We'll initiate campaigns to draw people in (a.k.a. grow our church attendance numbers) and try to help them conform to our church culture. Trust me. They see us for who we are, and when they don't see love in us, it's not their fault; it's ours. This obstacle must come down.

As I write this, I'm reminded of one of the most beautiful truths in God's Word. This is our number one message, and if we want to love like Jesus, this is how we must behave:

What do you think? If a man owns a hundred sheep, and one of them wanders away, will he not leave the ninety-nine on the hills and go look for the one that wandered off? (Matthew 18:12).

The shepherd Jesus refers to in this parable had to feel tremendous love and concern for that one wandering sheep; otherwise, he wouldn't leave his flock or the comfort of his campfire. I don't believe the sheepherder is motivated by irritation or the potential loss of income from one missing member of his flock. Compassion compelled the man to search for the lone lost sheep.

It's understandable to feel something other than love when we see kids acting out and being disrespectful, but the message Jesus proclaims is loud and clear. Jesus Himself tells us to *"not despise one of these little ones"* (or less mature) (v. 10). Each individual sheep is important to Him and deserves His love. And ours. I pray each of us asks Jesus to fill us with this same kind of love—His love—for all the lost sheep in our younger generations. May He teach us to bite our tongue, ignore some of the things that get under our skin, and go out of our way to show them the kindness and acceptance of Jesus that they so desperately need.

ROADBLOCK & OBSTACLE 2: THEY DON'T TRUST AUTHORITY

The Enemy has done an effective job of convincing young people to fight authority. He is using this to tear down institutions, whether it be family, church, or government.

As Christians, especially parents and grandparents, we tend

to fall into two camps on authority: We either wield it with fierce determination or we lean too far into grace and become overly permissive and accepting. Churches make rules, whether written or unspoken, that leaders sometimes do and sometimes don't enforce or follow. And our government... I don't want to even get started on the failed use of authority there. Our mixed messages of authority paint a confusing picture of what authority is supposed to look like. They've seen too much abuse of power and failure in leadership. This is why they resist the systems and leadership of those who have controlled their world up until now. They prefer to live independently and develop their own ways of doing things.

Truth is, the younger generations don't trust authority, not even in the church. Only 30% of Gen Z believe pastors have high standards of moral and ethics or trust pastors to do the right thing.[17] That means 70% of them drive past our churches and they think, *I can't trust them; That is not a safe place for me.* Now, I'm not saying 30% of pastors are untrustworthy. In fact, most are respectable leaders who are walking faithfully with God, godly people I'd gladly place my trust in. The point here is that the younger generations aren't seeing it. They've seen too many high-profile pastors exposed or local church leadership called out for inappropriate behavior. How many times have we seen

17. Earls, A. (2024, January 24). Public Trust of Pastors Hits New Record Low. Lifeway Research. http://research.lifeway.com/2024/01/24/public-trust-of-pastors-hits-new-record-low/

someone in a position of spiritual leadership get caught doing something they should not be doing? It doesn't matter how much we try to tell kids not all church people are villains; they've seen enough to be wary. As a result, the model of the church has taken a hit. This is why I advocate for promoting Jesus as kind, loving, sacrificial, Lord first—trustworthy—instead of feverishly promoting the local church that you love. This generation is very open to all Jesus offers, but turned off by the untrustworthy authority that much of the local church and spiritual leaders are known for.

ROADBLOCK & OBSTACLE 3: THEIR PERCEPTION OF CHURCH

One of the obstacles preventing young adults from finding Jesus is their perception of the church. That is a *huge* roadblock for young people. What Jesus offers is very attractive to them, but that doesn't equate to the church in their eyes. A recent study shows 70% of Millennials and Gen Z believe the American church is irrelevant.[18] They don't hate it; they just don't see a purpose in it.

And we don't go to places that don't serve a purpose.

For example, if you don't like fish, a sushi restaurant is irrelevant in your list of choices of where to go for dinner. You have no purpose to go there. The sushi bar is irrelevant to you. Here's another way to look at this: I have not gone to a laundromat since I bought a washing machine and our family can wash our

---

18. Rainer, T., & Rainer, J. (2009). The Millennials: Connecting to America's Largest Generation. B&H Publishing Group.

laundry in our own home. For us, the laundromat is irrelevant to our lives. Our younger generations simply feel no need for the church. It is irrelevant to them. They don't believe they need church. And that is sometimes redefined as not needing God either. The church and God are synonymous to the unchurched who haven't discovered an intimate relationship with Jesus. The church, and God by association, in their perspective are irrelevant.

The church no longer represents the heart of the community, a safe refuge for those in need or a place to find friends and peace and Jesus Himself. Only 34% of Gen Z believes churches have a positive impact on society, compared to 55% of Baby Boomers.[19] Instead, our kids see the church as judgmental, non-loving, untrustworthy, and full of meaningless rules. They're missing the point completely, and it's mostly our fault. We have constructed a church culture to which one belongs and complies with the expectations. That's not at all what Jesus describes as the body of Christ. The younger generations are building a life of their own and have convinced themselves they can figure it out. They have no interest in an irrelevant church.

ROADBLOCK & OBSTACLE 4: CONTROL

When young people look at the Christian community, they don't see the compassion and all the beautiful things that Jesus

19. Cox, Daniel A. (2024) "Generation Z and the Future of Faith in America"; https://www.americansurveycenter.org/research/generation-z-future-of-faith/

offers, because all they see are the restrictions and the rules. They don't understand the beauty of a relationship with Jesus like we older generations do because all they see is the control.

The True Message

In Mark 5, we read the story of a desperate man with an impure spirit. This man lived outside of town in the tombs, and he was cutting himself and crying out. Nobody knew what to do with him. The Bible says the man was often chained hand and foot, but then he would always break the chains and go back to the tombs. (See Mark 5:2–5.)

As I was pondering that story one day, I wondered… How do you chain up somebody? How do you tie up somebody who is so strong they can break anything you tie them up with?

And I had an answer: They have to volunteer.

In that moment, I pictured a modern-day scene of a desperate young person in our demographic. They're lost. They're broken. They're struggling. They're in turmoil, trying to make sense of life. They are craving peace and purpose, but they don't know where to find it.

Then one day this young person walks past a little church—I envisioned a little white steeple church in a small town—and they remember, *My grandma said that place could help me.* So they walk into the church and ask the first person they see, *"Hey, can you help me? I'm in pain and I don't know what to do."*

The only thing the church was equipped to offer them was

control. So the young person is told, *"Cut your hair. Change your clothes. Do things this way. Don't behave that way."* And out of a strong desire to find peace internally, they submit to this external control. They allow themselves to be tied up because they are so desperate for help.

But after some time has passed, the young person realizes the external controls aren't taking care of their internal struggle, the reason they sought help inside the church in the first place. So they break the chains and declare, *"I'm not sticking around for this."* And they go back to their modern-day tombs—their bad behavior, their addictions, their poor relationships—where they cut themselves and cry out in ways their generations understand, but we do not. The controls at the church didn't work, because the church wasn't offering Jesus.

But then all of a sudden, Jesus shows up in front of the hurting young person. And when Jesus shows up, His love is direct, heart to heart. He brings peace, hope, love, joy, fruit of the Spirit, everything the young person is needing, including eternal life. The young person falls to their knees in surrender, responding directly to Jesus' loving presence. That's what our young people need. It's what we all need.

The man in the tombs who had been cutting himself and crying out finally saw hope when he noticed Jesus get off the boat. *"When he saw Jesus from a distance, he ran and fell on his knees in front of him"* (Mark 5:6). The mercy Jesus showed the man changed him dramatically and drove out the demons. Jesus told the man, *"Go home to your own people and tell them how much the Lord has done for you, and how he has had mercy on you"* (v. 19). Jesus offers this same hope and mercy to all of us, including to the younger generations who are being tormented by the Enemy in today's culture.

One of the aspects of this story I find interesting is that once the wild man was transformed and *"dressed and in his right mind,"* (v 15) the people were afraid. They begged Jesus to leave the region. I wonder if the townspeople got so used to this tormented man's screaming and self-cutting—way out in the tombs and outside the safety of their town, mind you—that this "new man" in their midst made them uncomfortable. He didn't fit into their local community bubble.

It seems to me this still happens today. Our neat and tidy churches are uncomfortable around these young people who come in from the tombs, transformed by Jesus and on fire for Him. With fresh zeal, and sometimes untraditional style and ungodly pasts, these kids shine light into our dusty Christian lives. They want to change the world, but we've grown accustomed to the way things are.

The truth is, we need God's mercy every day just as much as these hurting young people do. Jesus wants us to *"go tell how much the Lord has done"* for us, and *"how He has had mercy"* on us, just like He instructed the man in the tombs. We should be inspired by the ones Jesus is contending for, not distancing ourselves from them because they make us uncomfortable. Or worse, holding them at bay because they're not "cleaned up" enough yet.

> Lift up the rewards of relationship; they don't respond well to the rules of religion.

Let's look closely at our message. What are we communicating? Are we reminding the younger generations there is a God in heaven who desperately loves them and desires to encourage them? Do we share that He created them intentionally and knows what He put inside of them—things that will bring them joy and fulfillment as they walk with Him? And are we telling them that God desires to spend eternity with them in heaven and made a way that is possible? I encourage each of us to lift up the rewards of relationship with Jesus because the younger generations don't respond well to the rules of religion. Instead, let us choose to lead with grace, mercy, and compassion, trusting the Holy Spirit to draw them in, convict them, and transform them. Some people may think young people are unreachable, but Jesus can get through to them in the midst of their confusion and pain. He is our message, and He is enough.

CHAPTER 4

They Are Waiting

When he saw the crowds, he had compassion on them, because they were harassed and helpless, like sheep without a shepherd. Then he said to his disciples, "The harvest is plentiful but the workers are few" (Matthew 9:36–37).

MILLENNIALS AND Gen Z need the message of Jesus. They want what He has to offer. They are hiding out in their modern-day tombs, hurting themselves and crying out, and they are waiting for someone to introduce them to Jesus.

At the height of Jesus' ministry, He traveled across Galilee teaching His message and healing the sick. His disciple Matthew lists story after story of Jesus touching lepers, restoring sight to the blind, hearing to the deaf, life to the dead. Everywhere He went, crowds of sick and hurting people came to Him for help.

We read in Matthew 9:35–36 that *"Jesus went through all the towns and villages, teaching in their synagogues, proclaiming the good news of the kingdom and healing every disease and sickness. When he saw the crowds, he had compassion on them, because they were harassed and helpless, like sheep without a shepherd."*

In Matthew's detailed notes, we see more than a checklist of healings. We see a desperate generation, a loving Savior, and a monumental opportunity that calls on each of us.

Culture is a Mess

This account from Matthew identifies what Jesus saw in the culture of His day. As He walked through the crowds from town to town, He observed the crowds were *"harassed and helpless, like sheep without a shepherd."* The people didn't know who to trust. They didn't know who was lying, who was telling the truth. They were abandoned with no guidance they could place their trust in. He had compassion, because when Jesus looked at His day's culture, He saw the mess they were in. They were harassed. Helpless.

I think that's a good way to describe our culture right now. More than any other time in my life, I believe the younger generations in our world today are in the same condition as what Jesus saw two thousand years ago. Millennials and Gen Z are harassed and helpless like sheep without a shepherd. Young people don't know who to trust. They don't know which religion is telling the truth. They don't know which political party is telling the truth. They wonder: Is the church telling me the truth? Is the world telling me the truth? Is the right telling me the truth? Is the left? They don't know if they trust their parents anymore. More often than not, they trust their peers more than they trust their parents or authority figures.

Today's culture is indeed a mess. And I don't necessarily think that only applies to those who are unchurched. We have made some mistakes inside our church culture and messed it up as well. Unless we submit to Jesus as our Shepherd, we are also harassed and helpless. We can either sit back and point our fingers at a messed up people, or we can focus our eyes on Jesus and ask Him to help make sense of the mess trying to dominate our view. He will train us to make a difference. With compassion. With urgency. With purpose to draw the messed up people to Himself, inside and outside the church.

Open and Hungry

Jesus made a bold statement in Matthew 9:37 when he said, *"The harvest is plentiful."* He conveyed in that moment that when people are confused and struggling and don't know who to trust, they are more open to the gospel than when everything is going great in their life. When the culture is a mess, when people don't know who to trust, they are more open to the gospel. Sometimes their behavior or postures indicate they're not open, but they are.

That is what is happening today. I believe there is a massive move of young people waking up in the morning, saying, *"Man, the rug has been ripped out from under me. I don't know what my future is going to look like. I have no security. I have no stability."* They're looking for something, someone, to trust. That's why what Jesus offers is so attractive, the gospel so appealing. The younger generations are hungry for hope, purpose, peace, joy, and everything He offers.

Barry Meguiar shares in his book, *Ignite Your Life*,[20] that the vast majority of the unchurched would like to believe there's a God who can make sense out of today's chaos, and they're looking for someone to tell them who that God is. I'm seeing the same thing through my encounters with kids around the country. The spiritual harvest is *plentiful*. There are countless young people willing to welcome God's promises of salvation, ready to embrace God's Rescue Plan and to surrender to His grace. The problem is they don't know how to ask for it.

What We Can Do

In this passage, Jesus goes on to say that there aren't enough laborers in the field. *"Then he said to his disciples, 'The harvest is plentiful but the workers are few'"* (v. 38). To put that in today's language, there are too few Baby Boomers and Gen X actively pursuing the younger generations to connect them to Jesus. There aren't enough mature adults who are thinking about the harvest, not enough hands to gather the fullness of what God wants to bring in.

The harvest is plentiful but the workers are few. I've wrestled with that passage because if that's true, and we know it is because Jesus said so, it flips our Christian paradigm on its head. It means we're not waiting for them; they're waiting for us. And most of us don't seem to be budging.

20. Barry Maguire, Ignite Your Life, (Charisma House, February 2023)

Two decades ago, after reading this passage in Matthew 9, I sat at my desk and scribbled out a question on a Post-it Note. I stuck it in my Bible and kept it there for years.

The question was simply this: Is it possible they are more willing to consider and respond to the claims of Christ than we, as the church, are willing and equipped to go share with them?

It's a tough question to ponder. And here's what I have realized. As Christians, we are not expected to do the work God calls us to without Him. Jesus points this out clearly, but in our rush, we might miss it. He follows up his statement about not having enough workers with a prayer request in the next verse. *"Ask the Lord of the harvest, therefore, to send out workers into his harvest field"* (v. 39). Of course! We pray. We see consistently throughout God's Word how He prepares His people before they embark on a big assignment from Him, and we see repeatedly how He empowers them to accomplish it. We are never alone in our obedience to what God is calling us to do. God is always with us. Our responsibility is to rely on Him.

Jesus knew what He was doing when He told the disciples to ask God to send out workers, because He knows the power and the benefits of prayer, of surrendered closeness to the Father, intimacy with Jesus and the Holy Spirit.

In our Christian bubble, we have convinced ourselves that the emerging generations are not interested in what Jesus offers, but could it be that the problem is not with them, but with us?

One of the reasons the older generations have problems connecting is because internally, many of us aren't living as intimately with the Lord as we could. We get distracted with the stuff of life. And quite honestly, if we don't keep pressing into our relationship with Jesus, the flame of our first love for Him becomes as worn out as an over sung song that drags on with no life. And as a result, we don't communicate the renewing love of Jesus well.

What we need is a renewal of our heart and spirit. That happens when we spend intentional, honest time alone with God. Quite often we pursue community more than we pursue Christ. We crave the satisfaction and comfort of human friendships more than intimacy in our time with Jesus. Yes, our community is an important part of walking in our faith. The Bible teaches a clear message about the importance of the body of Christ. We benefit from a relationship with other Christians. But we also need intimate time with God, just Him and us.

Spiritually, we're stunted if we avoid solitude. The most powerful part of our day is when we draw away and say, *"God, here I am. I'm opening Your Word. I need You to speak to me. I need to focus my attention on You. I want to draw close to You because I know then You'll draw close to me. And as I draw close to You, I know that You'll transform me from the inside out. You're going to help me overcome. You're going to strengthen me in areas where I'm weak. You're going to give me courage in areas where I'm starting to be fearful."* It's that private place that impacts us and that we have to run after so we can fulfill the role God is calling us to. In solitude is where we are built up in our faith. God builds you in private to use you in public.

God builds you in private to use you in public.

As mature Christians and as the older generations, we need to be careful to not just go through the motions, but to truly continue running after Christ. Let Him transform you and teach you and mold you and shape you and sculpt you on an ongoing basis in an ongoing way. Not only will that benefit you greatly in your personal faith, but it gives you the God-powered ability to impact the generations who are coming up next. Our job is to lift up the name of Jesus, knowing that He meets the needs of everyone who looks to Him. We're more inclined to do our job when we're overflowing with His love from time spent alone with Him.

Three Basic Truths

Everywhere I go, I remind people of these three basic truths. If our Christian community would embrace these truths, fervently believe them and act on them, our world would be a much better place.

Consider these three simple, basic truths:

1. God is still good.
2. The gospel is still powerful.
3. The harvest is still ripe.

I think we can all agree that most Christians believe God is good when circumstances are good. But do we really believe God is good when we get bad news, when something doesn't go our way, when a dream is broken, when a relationship is struggling? Even then, God is still good.

The second truth is that the gospel is still powerful. Do we really believe that's true? Do we look across the yard at certain neighbors or coworkers in the office and long for them to know the good news of the gospel? When I was in high school, I had a kind of antihero. He was a jock, and I actually thought he didn't need God since he already had everything going for him, in my opinion. I thought he would reject the love and grace of Jesus because he operated with arrogance and carried himself with a barrier that implied he was in control. Now I see how wrong I was. A few years after graduating from high school, someone shared Jesus with him and he surrendered. He is now one of the most on fire Christian men I know. This taught me, in a very real and personal way, that the gospel truly is powerful. Jesus can break through any wall and reach any heart.

Can you relate? Are there people in your life who you think will never respond to Jesus? Some who are so hard they can never be reached? Perhaps you think God can't break through their hardened hearts, their self-sufficiency, their pride, their whatever-it-is. The gospel hasn't changed. It is still as powerful and transformational as the very moment Jesus stepped out of that tomb.

The third truth is that the harvest is still ripe, as we've already been discussing in this chapter. I've had people tell me, "I don't see it in the USA. Therefore, I don't know that I believe it for here. I believe it over there in Asia, in Africa, where people are coming to Jesus. I believe it over there, but not closer to home."

But I have seen that young people are indeed hungry for the

gospel here in the USA. People, even Millennials and Gen Z, are more open to the gospel right now than they've ever been before. They're just waiting for somebody to come and share that truth with them.

So let me ask you… "Is it possible that they (those who are lost and alone) are more willing to consider and respond to the message of Christ, than we (Christ followers) are willing and equipped to share Him?" The answer is YES. But together we can see that change.

> God will take an ordinary person and use them in extraordinary ways.

Do we believe that God is still good? Do we believe that the gospel is still powerful? Do we believe the harvest is still ripe? Yes? Then we're already on our way to being able to reach the next generations.

God is looking for laborers. He wants us to pray that He would raise these workers up, but He is also inviting us to join the team. The question isn't if God will use us, but will we follow Him into the fields?

You might say, *"I don't know what to say,"* or perhaps, *"I don't have anything to offer."* That is okay. God will take "ordinaries" (from Chapter 1) and use them in extraordinary ways. Your job is to be a willing vessel; His job is to break through. And God has been breaking through since the beginning of time. No heart is too hard, no soul too dry. No mind is too far gone. His Holy Spirit

53

can do a renewing work in every generation, both old and new.

"I will give you a new heart and put a new spirit in you; I will remove from you your heart of stone and give you a heart of flesh" (Ezekiel 36:26).

Will you pray with me for the Lord of the harvest to raise up laborers to go into the harvest field? And will you volunteer for service?

The situation is the same today as it was when Jesus walked the earth and found the culture messed up, the harvest ripe, and laborers few. Can we begin to live with these three premises that God is still good, that the gospel is still powerful, and that the harvest is still ripe? We're seeing it everywhere. Groundwire is not the only place that we're seeing young people coming to Jesus. You may have heard it from other ministries as well. There is a movement of God among people in our nation.

Remember, according to Jesus, we are not waiting on them. They are waiting on us.

Crossing the Street

Before God led us down the path of leveraging media and technology to share Jesus, I was speaking to 150,000 people a year. As God began to transition my heart, I realized my ministry was built around an invitation.

The Scriptures say to go. Jesus told the disciples, *"Go into all the world and preach the gospel to all creation"* (Mark 16:15).

He said, "Go." And I kept saying, "Come."

I was asking them to come where they don't want to be. We already know Gen Z and Millennials believe the American church is irrelevant. Their negative view of church makes it unrealistic to think the majority will step inside one in search of truth.

In order to scale and reach an audience that won't walk through church doors, we need to change our approach. The old model of *"Let's get them to a building where they can hear about the Man"* is going through a serious mind shift. Now we say, *"Let's tell them about the Man and then move them toward the church."* The goal is not to get them into church. The goal is to introduce them to Jesus, see them accept His saving grace, then move them into Christian community. But they're not going to walk into the church and say, *"Hey, I got questions."* They're not going to approach a Christian and say, *"Hey, I want to get saved."*

Yet because they don't come to us, we think they are not interested. We think they are not willing. We sit behind our church walls and our programs, and we look at culture and we think if they have questions, surely they will show up on Sunday morning. Surely they will walk through our door and they will ask the right question. They will say, *"Hey, I am in need. Would you help me?"* Surely they will do that, we think.

All the while, the culture sits across the street and they look at us and they think, *"If you've got the answer, surely you will come tell me. If you can tell me where to find peace and hope and inner healing and purpose, then surely you will share those things with me. Please come and step into my life and engage with me and help me."*

And unfortunately, nobody is crossing the street.

Recently, however, I heard about someone who did.

In April 2024, a nationwide call led hundreds of Christians to gather at State Capitols across the nation. The rally was titled "Call to the Capitol." The purpose was for Christians to gather in fellowship and to protest against LGBTQ ideology, especially transgender policies and teaching, showing up in public schools. At my local State Capitol in Denver, speakers took turns sharing their Christian perspective on this controversial issue while hundreds of attendees applauded and cheered at the message onstage.

In their own protest to the Christian gathering, the transgender community was camped out across the street at Liberty Park. The crowd of mostly young people sat on blankets or stood as close as they could get to the edge of the street, watching the Christians on the other side. The trans community played their own music and held signs in protest, making a non-aggressive stand.

At one point, a Gen X pastor's wife crossed the street. She walked over to the transgender side and stood toward the back of the group, watching, perhaps praying and waiting for an opportunity to talk with some of the trans participants. One of the transgender individuals made eye contact with this Christian woman. They smiled and waved at each other, and started talking. Their conversation began with a discussion about the political divide on each side of the street, then eventually ended up going deep and honest.

The pastor's wife asked sincere questions that came from true concern. She asked this transgender Millennial if the transgender peers of her generation hated God and Christianity. The trans person explained how so many members of their community have suffered personal trauma from the church. They have also seen the hypocrisy of Christians, something this group that values authenticity just can't embrace. As a pastor's wife, this woman had seen firsthand the unkindness of Christians toward the transgender community. She shared with her new transgender friend how she grieves when people sit in church listening to sermons about peace and love, then pour out of the church only to express meanness and unkindness toward those who hold different beliefs.

The conversation between these two people from opposite sides of the street lasted for an hour.

Then another woman crossed the street from the Christian side. She approached the transgender crowd with a dour look on her face and a combative attitude. She beelined to the same transgender individual who was talking with the pastor's wife and immediately launched into Christian dialect. "How can you have a personal relationship with God if you're choosing to live in sin?" and "Have you been feasting on the Word of God?" Her questions were filled with judgment and disapproval. She started arguing about right and wrong, telling them how they were all wrong. When she could tell she wasn't getting anywhere, she spouted, "Have a blessed day" and stormed off to confront another protestor.

The pastor's wife expressed an apology for the bad behavior of the so-called Christian belligerent woman. The trans person explained this is how these types of conversations usually go—

Christians hurling insults or judgment at their community.

The love, peace, and hope found in Jesus is exactly what these young people are longing for. Unfortunately, when judgmental Christians get in the way, the next generations turn and run. Jesus tells us the harvest is ripe and to pray for laborers. He wasn't appointing us to cross the street to tell them how wrong they were. We need to stop looking at what they're doing wrong, and we need to start pointing them to the One who's always right. That is a message they will respond to.

Meanwhile, at the protest rally, the confrontation between the "Have a blessed day" protestor and her LGBTQ target, who was wearing blatant Satanic paraphernalia, turned hostile almost immediately. The situation between the Christian and the Satan follower escalated, bringing the pastor's wife's positive conversation to an end. Her transgender friend went to pull the angry LGBTQ community member away from the angry Christian, while the pastor's wife escorted her Christian sister back to the other side of the street.

Then the most surprising and wonderful thing happened. The pastor's wife crossed the street again.

She approached the Satanist and apologized to her for the other Christian's behavior and extended the loving hand of Jesus from across the street. She also approached the Millennial transgender she'd been conversing with, expressed her appreciation for their meaningful conversation, and the two exchanged contact information so they could continue their newfound friendship.

Let's get to the real issue here. If you know how to speak to a subject like the LGBTQ community, the abortion issue, or some other cultural hot spot, but you don't know how to bring light and hope and Jesus into these situations, it's incomplete at best. A disastrous turnoff to lost souls at worst. Before we start arguing the issues, we must capture the heart of what we're dealing with. And without hellfire and brimstone. Let's show people the life-transforming love of Jesus.

That's what I mean when I talk about crossing the street—openly, lovingly, purposefully going out of our way to share the love of Jesus with the younger generations, differences and all. With the compassion of Jesus for a generation that is harassed and helpless, sheep without a shepherd. I'm inspired to cross the street like this pastor's wife did, and I hope you are too.

It's so clear young people are open to the message of Jesus. They're just not going to come to us to hear it. We know Christ can answer their questions. We know that whether they need purpose, hope, peace, joy… whether it's love and acceptance… all of those things come through Christ, as does eternity with Him.

The culture is a mess. The harvest is ripe. Laborers are few. Will we go?

CHAPTER 5

The Time Is Now

"Come, follow me," Jesus said, "and I will send you out to fish for people" (Matthew 4:19).

ALTHOUGH I can't find an official source, I have heard church and denominational leaders say that the average church in the US sees one person a year give their life to Christ. Keep in mind, this is an average. There are several dynamic churches across the country that are seeing significantly higher numbers. That means there are many who aren't seeing any at all. How many of our churches are ministering to the same group of individuals year after year? No new people coming to Jesus, no new believers joining their ranks. Thankfully, vibrant churches with an evangelistic focus are carrying the load for the rest of us. But the result is still a church average of one new believer per year.

As sad as this truth is, I don't believe it is completely the church's fault. Rather, this dismal statistic reflects our current culture's disinterest in the church. Not surprisingly, this lack of interest is amplified among the younger generations. Note: I did not say a disinterest in Jesus, but the organized gatherings we call church.

Because we learned to lead with Jesus, Groundwire is miraculously seeing hundreds of thousands a year make that commitment. The numbers topped one million for the first time in 2024. I don't share this to brag about our ministry; I share it to show there is a way that works. We aren't waiting for them to come find us; we are crossing the street and discovering hungry, ripe, hurting young people who want the peace and healing that Jesus offers.

> Young people are more open to the gospel, to considering and responding to the claims of Christ right now more than ever.

Young people are more open to the gospel, to considering and responding to the claims of Christ right now more than ever—since I've been alive and, I believe, even in the history of our nation.

Over the past 200 years, the United States has experienced a handful of significant revivals. In the early 1800s three college students in Virginia sparked a revival through their refusal to stop praying and reading the Bible in their dorm room, and in the mid 1800s noonday prayer saw thousands gathering daily in New York City, deepening the faith of many and seeing many turn to Jesus.[21] Many Baby Boomers witnessed firsthand the impact of

---

21. https://developingkingdomleaders.com/2023/02/27/revivals-in-america/

the Jesus Movement in the 1960s and '70s. All of these revivals were centered around a university, a city, or a specific gathering. What we're seeing today is different. The spiritual hunger among our young people today is not relegated to a location or event; today the hunger is everywhere.

The Jesus movement saw 250,000 people choose to follow Him.[22] Today we are seeing a significantly greater harvest—in every state, city, ethnicity, and socioeconomic class. This movement isn't just a certain type of people (college students) who are turning to Jesus; it is happening with thousands of young people everywhere in every class. Behind the masks, everyone is searching for the solutions.

That's why I believe we're seeing the high numbers of next gens accepting Jesus. I believe the potential for widespread revival is greater today because of the palpable emptiness, loneliness, and hopelessness among Millennials and Gen Z. We are seeing a greater spiritual openness and interest in spiritual growth than ever before. Barna research shows 77% of Gen Z say they are open to the existence of God or a higher power or express curiosity about spiritual matters. And 74% of Gen Z says they want to grow spiritually, showing that despite cultural challenges, there's a hunger for deeper faith experiences.[23] The younger generations

---

22. https://developingkingdomleaders.com/2023/02/27/revivals-in-america/

23. Kinnaman, David. (2024) "Rising Spiritual Openness in America" https://www.barna.com/research/rising-spiritual-openness/

are searching for something to fill that unavoidable hole in their heart. Recent revivals on college campuses further show there's a spiritual hunger among our youth.

Looking again at the message Jesus shares in Matthew 9:35–38 supports this observation. The kids in our culture are "harassed and helpless". When the rug of comfort, direction, confidence, has been ripped out, young people are willing to consider other solutions that bring them hope, peace, joy. They are inundated with hopelessness and unanswerable questions.

Their hopelessness makes them ponder:

Is the American Dream possible? Will I ever achieve any kind of financial stability and be able to afford a secure life?

Will I ever be able to overcome my addictions?

Can I ever have a healthy and long-lasting relationship?

Will I ever fit in and feel safe?

Out of control emotions fill their minds, and they wonder:

Will I ever have peace?

Will I ever be without paralyzing anxiety?

The world is unsafe. When is tragedy going to hit me?

Suicide has become more normalized within the younger generations. They are watching people they love take their own lives, and they scramble to understand, crying, *What is going on?*

They want to have a purpose in life, but at the same time they feel they could never have a purpose of great enough value. They think, *I want to make a difference, but will I ever be able to make a significant contribution?*

Then they wrap it all up in a bow of comparison, convinced they're the only ones struggling. Why am I the only one left out? Why is everyone living their best life when I am stuck in a miserable life?

To sum it up, young people are confused and miserable. Because of that… The harvest is ripe.

So, we know there's a tremendous need and an openness to the truth that offers hope, and we hold the answer in Jesus, but how do we make the connection with the next generations so we can share the Good News?

Let's first talk about a young girl we'll call Sara. As you look at Sara's exterior and demeanor, you may assume she would not be open to a conversation about Jesus or faith. Sara rolls her eyes at anything "church" or "Jesus" related. Her favorite holiday is Halloween, and she scoffs at Columbus Day and Thanksgiving because of the injustice to Indigenous people. She wears pins and badges on her clothing that spout popular worldviews, like "My body, My choice" and "Create your own truth" and you wonder how in the world you could ever get through to her. Don't let the appearances and the broadcasted messages fool you. Sara doesn't wake up every morning asking spiritual questions. She is in survival mode, just like the majority of her generation.

What we need to remember is that behind her mask, Sara is crying out for everything Jesus offers. She is craving hope and longing for peace. She wants to know that she is valuable and that life will get better. That desire is the doorway that leads to a meaningful conversation about Jesus, and the conversation begins when someone connects with her pain and listens to her internal cry. When Sara feels listened to, she, in turn, is willing to listen. When Sara feels safe and unthreatened, she is open to hearing about the God in heaven who loves her and has a plan for her life. When Sara hears about His unconditional love for her, about Jesus' desire for her to have peace and purpose, in that moment, the "God conversation" becomes relevant. It isn't a debate on theology, it is a practical, relational, appealing discussion about the benefits of everything Jesus offers. And when Sara sees the truth, she prays to receive Christ and excitedly begins her new journey with Him. Sara's journey to a personal relationship with Jesus all begins with someone like you or me pursuing a connection with her.

> **They are looking for answers; they just don't know how to articulate the questions.**

Each of us knows someone like Sara. They have different names and live in different towns and wear different messages on their clothes and backpacks. They might be a family member or someone in your neighborhood, may even be your daughter or son or grandchild. They may live down the street or down the hall.

Sara represents the many lost and broken young people who are struggling. Their pain is intense; their unspoken questions deafening. The truth is, they are looking for answers; they just don't know how to articulate the questions. We have to help them ask the right questions, the questions that really matter. That can only happen once we establish a connection with them.

Being Intentional

The Millennials and Gen Z in your life, perhaps your kids and grandkids, are near and dear to your heart, but you worry about them. You want them to know Jesus personally. You want them to understand that He cares about them deeply and has a plan for their life. You want them to know that He offers peace in a crazy world and hope in dark times, but those conversations are so difficult to have.

I understand how discouraging this can feel to a caring adult. When the young person we care about clings openly to ungodly views or avoids talking about faith, it can feel hopeless. We might find ourselves asking almost in vain, *"What can I do?"* Against popular opinion, we older adults can do a lot to influence the next generations. We know what they are searching for, even if they don't. All the questions and angst they are struggling with can be resolved in a day-to-day walk in surrender to Jesus.

So, what can we do? We can intentionally connect with them in conversation. I know this can sometimes feel daunting… impossible even, but I'm going to show you how to steer the conversation toward matters of faith in an organic and non-controversial manner. Here are some steps to help you prepare.

RAISE YOUR SPIRITUAL ANTENNA.

To raise up your spiritual antenna, first quiet yourself in prayer. Make this a priority daily. As you pursue God and begin your day with a posture of submission and surrender, ask God to heighten your senses to those in need around you and to use you to introduce all that Jesus offers to a hurting generation. Pray and ask God to get you ready. Then listen. When you listen to the Holy Spirit's whispers, He will help you identify the young people in your life He wants you to connect with. He knows exactly who you can encourage and help. He'll lead you, not only to the hurting person but also in connecting with them. When your spiritual antenna is raised and tuned in, the Holy Spirit will tell you when and how to start a conversation.

This all starts in your "quiet place" with God and continues as you live in the chaotic activity of your day. Continue to keep your eyes and ears open. God will nudge you. He will direct your attention to a stranger, or you will slow down in your neighborhood at the sight of someone you've been meaning to talk to, as God moves your heart. When that happens, say a quick prayer and then step out.

ENGAGE IN OPENING CONVERSATIONS.

Recently, my wife, Jené, and I were in a busy restaurant on a Saturday night. Our server was running, but we wanted her to know that we saw her and we cared about her.

So I interjected, "I know you are busy and you don't have a

lot of time to chat, but I wanted you to know that my goal for the evening is that when it's all said and done, we were your favorite table of the evening."

She smiled. "You already are. You are the only table that asked me questions and wanted to know something about my life."

This brief exchange reinforced my strong opinion that people are willing to answer questions and want to be heard.

When trying to get past someone's barriers, don't do all of the talking. Ask meaningful questions. There is something in most of us that believe our opinions need to be heard. The problem is that many people don't care what you have to say until they personally feel you have listened to them. Because of that, asking the right questions can move your conversations in the right direction.

Ask questions that show you are genuinely interested. Pay attention to what the young person is wearing, carrying, representing. Is he wearing a sports jersey? Ask about his team and how they are doing. If you notice a bass clef tattoo on a girl's arm, ask her about it. Does she play an instrument? How did she get into that? What are her goals, her challenges? Keep the conversation friendly and productive.

Admitting that times have been crazy and then asking how they have been impacted is a great tactic. Ask them about their generation and how they are coping with anxiety and disappointment. When you ask the questions, be sure to listen to their answers. They will give you a glimpse into the areas where they are struggling.

To prevent walls from going up or making these conversations uncomfortable, fight the urge to react when they talk about something you hate. Instead, steer the focus to what you believe in. The Christian community has a reputation for being angry and judgmental. Culture says, *"We know what they hate, but we really don't know what they stand for."* Use these conversations to gently show what you stand for. Talk about goodness and kindness without complaining about the political trends the young person might embrace. Don't tell them what you think they should be doing or point out what they are doing wrong, but share what God is doing in the world around you. They may look disinterested, but they are paying attention. They want to believe in hope.

Before ending these opening conversations, ask them, *"How can I support you? How can I be praying for you?"* The majority of young people have tangible anxiety and stress, and if approached correctly will welcome this type of support.

When appropriate, be sure to follow up, especially if you see pain and brokenness in the eyes and responses of someone close to you, like a child or grandchild. These opening conversations can be an ideal jumping-off point for deeper discussions. Discipline yourself to follow up. Follow-up does not come naturally for most of us. Text the next day to ask how the interview or sports event went, how their day was, or to remind them you are praying for them. This intentional show of interest and concern will go a long way toward building long-term trust and even more meaningful conversations in the future.

ASK GOD FOR DISCERNMENT.

Connecting in conversations will reveal where kids stand on many things, including spiritual. I encourage you to ask God regularly to help you see beyond the masks that are projected and see the pain of those you come in contact with. The younger generations want us to think they're doing just fine, and they will spin their words to make themselves appear confident and self-sufficient. As you talk with them, pray for discernment to be able to see through the smokescreen. Ask God to show you what is authentic and what is an attempt to cover their pain. When God reveals their struggle, your compassion will increase and your ability to connect with them will grow.

BE AUTHENTIC.

Millennials and Gen Z know what posers look like, and they won't hesitate to walk out on you if they feel you are being inauthentic. They want real. If you fake a smile or give false praise, they'll recognize it immediately. Nothing will turn them off, and away, quicker than someone trying to be someone or something they're not, especially if it's in an attempt to impress or persuade. Kids do not respond well to preachy, but if they see you loving Jesus, serving others, and authentically interested in them, they will pay attention to you. They will even listen to how you share your faith. But only if you're being your true self with them. Millennials and Gen Z prefer "real" conversations and transparency when discussing faith, creating an opportunity for relational evangelism.

BE VULNERABLE.

Rather than preaching a mini-sermon and sharing your wisdom, give them a glimpse into your struggles. Identify with them on a level they can relate to. When they reveal they are feeling overwhelmed, unloved, or anxious, you can share, *"When I am feeling anxious, I..."* or *"When I was younger, I struggled with depression, but I found hope."* If they feel you can't relate and you don't care, they will tune you out, but if they feel you understand, they will lean in.

Share what God has been teaching you. Instead of telling them what you want them to hear, let them hear in you what they are looking for, but don't even realize it. *"I had some very difficult times this year, but I sensed God's presence and peace in a very tangible way."* Or, *"When I was overwhelmed earlier in the year, God reminded me that He is always with me and will never let me down."* Internally, they may argue whether or not God can meet their needs, but when they hear you tell your story, their doubts will start to give way.

I do want to caution you, however, that when you share your story, don't overdo it. Don't take the attention away from the other person by dominating the conversation with your historical narrative. Shifting the attention to yourself will make them feel you are not empathetic. Instead, connect through vulnerability, being sure to let them be the center of the conversation. When you connect Christ with their felt needs through your story, that's when they're willing to listen.

By being vulnerable, authentic, discerning, in tune with His leading, you will be able to connect in meaningful conversations, the first step toward leading a lost soul closer to Jesus. He is willing and able to heal their pain and offer them eternal life, and we can help connect the dots for them.

Today, you may bump into someone who is struggling, someone the Holy Spirit has put in your path. Stay alert. Stay focused on Jesus. Invite Him to use you and then don't back down. Your goal is to tell the Sara—or Justin, Addison, Connor, whatever the name of the young person in your life—that they were created to walk in relationship with God through Jesus, and it starts the day they say "yes" to Him.

CHAPTER 6

Earning the Right

We are therefore Christ's ambassadors, as though God were making his appeal through us. We implore you on Christ's behalf: Be reconciled to God (2 Corinthians 5:20).

TALKING ABOUT faith isn't a natural topic for most people. We know Jesus is the answer to all the heartache the younger generations are suffering, but we don't know how to connect, how to bring up the truth without being shut down. It feels threatening to share Jesus with a young person who seems so opposed to hearing about Him. Will they laugh at us? Get angry and tell us to back off or worse? I get it. I've had to learn how to navigate these conversations effectively myself. Over the years I've seen what works and what doesn't.

What Doesn't Work

When I was a teenager, I used to go street witnessing weekly with my youth group. On one particular occasion, I'd had a bad day, and I ambushed some poor guy with the truth. He was sitting at the bus stop, minding his own business, when I sat beside him. We chatted for a bit like you do when you're sitting on a bench waiting for the bus. Non-important stuff like the weather and will the bus be on time? The conversation went well until I brought up the topic of faith.

He gently said in a very kind way, "I'm just not interested in talking about faith or Jesus."

Rather than accept his polite refusal to move the conversation toward faith, I got mad. To be fully truthful, I just kind of lost it on him.

"You're miserable!" I snapped. Actually, I was the one who was miserable that day. But unfortunately I went on.

"You're searching for something and you're empty. You don't even know what it is."

And then I really went for it with a whopper of a line.

"If you want joy like me, you'll only find that in Jesus."

I said that last line almost sneering as I walked away. Looking back, I cringe at that miserable, bad experience. I hope God has redeemed my poor attempt at leading this poor man to Jesus by letting him encounter someone more mature in their faith, someone better equipped to share Jesus with kindness than I was at the time.

I made the mistake of focusing on my agenda, and that agenda was to get to the finish line as quickly as possible. I wanted the guy to know Jesus, and I ambushed him. I'm here to tell you that doesn't work. Perhaps you have experienced something similar. Sometimes when we finally get the opportunity to talk about faith, we're so eager to get this person to the finish line that we ambush them, as opposed to simply using niceties and engaging in conversation. Forcing our agenda doesn't work. Guiding the conversation in a friendly, organic way does.

What Does Work

Several years ago, I worked at a church in San Jose, California, and to supplement my income, I took a second job at an athletic club, which is kind of comical if you see me today. One of the trainers found out I also worked at a church, and he liked to tease me about it. He had ripped abs and drove a white Porsche convertible. I mean, he had it all together. He took pleasure in mocking me, and I just took it. I continued to befriend him and be kind. I'd make myself available, ask him how his day was going, and look for opportunities to interact with him.

At first, he continued to tease me for "believing that stuff" and living with conviction, because his priorities were completely different from mine. But he was lacking peace, joy, and hope. Even though he would never let anybody see it, he was guarding himself behind his fit and successful image. Over the next three or four months, he started to talk to me as a friend. Pretty soon that wall began to come down.

One day, as he was having lunch, I came out from behind the service counter and sat with him. I knew he was going through some stuff, and I didn't even have to bring it up.

He said, "Man, what's going on with you? You seem different."

So I shared honestly with him. "I know you think it's not real, but the truth of the matter is that God gives me peace and joy and hope."

He replied, "I'm really struggling right now with why I'm even here. My parents were religious and it just never made sense to me why somebody would trust somebody they can't see."

Throughout our conversation, he started to open up. He listened and he engaged. I shared about the authenticity of a relationship with Jesus—not the rules of religion, not the "you need to go to church."

I just said, "Hey, this is what's happened in my life. This is where I find purpose and hope and peace." I didn't ambush him or demand he surrender to Jesus. I just ended the conversation, and we both headed back to work.

Over the next couple days, he would just kind of linger around. We'd chat and sometimes talk more seriously about what he was going through and what Jesus is all about.

Around a week later, he asked me, "So what do I need to do to find that peace?"

"It begins with a personal relationship with Jesus," I answered. "It's not about joining the church; it's about submitting and surrendering your life to Jesus."

The authenticity and connection of our relationship—not my pushing, yelling, or forcing it on him—eventually led this coworker to a personal relationship with Jesus. When we take the time to be available and patiently connect in relationship, we open the doors for more receptivity.

Today, we have a massive team of Groundwire volunteers all over the world who engage with young people online and introduce them to Jesus. Gently, without ambushing them, and it's working. We train our online volunteers with the acronym L.E.T.S. to walk them through their conversations. This effective guideline will help all of us learn how to talk with the younger generations and gently lead them to Jesus.

L.E.T.S. stands for Listen, Empathize, Transition, and Share. This is our primary teaching tool to teach our coaches how to connect with our young audience and how to connect that audience to Jesus. The L.E.T.S. approach can be an effective tool for anyone with a passion to reach the next generations. I've had many people, even grandparents, say how much this simple acronym helped frame their conversations. Let's take a closer look (no pun intended).

L.E.T.S.

> L.E.T.S. stands for Listen, Empathize, Transition, and Share.

LISTEN

As the older generations, the number one change for us to make is to understand that talking *at* the younger generations doesn't work; dialoguing *with* them does. They are tired of the monologue they perceive coming from the church, but they are open to a dialogue—if we are sincere and open to listen to their side of the story. So instead of unleashing your wisdom on the young person, try to hear what they are saying and what remains unsaid.

When you ask questions to determine what they are feeling and struggling with, you will most likely discover they're very open to talking. Take time to hear what they are saying.

One of the problems is we sometimes don't listen. We just want to share. We're quick to jump in with, *"Let me tell you what you need."* Our words become dictatorial: you *should* or you *need to*… And it doesn't work.

> Talking at the younger generations doesn't work; dialoguing with them does.

But when we listen, we show one of the loving characteristics of God. He listens to us and He wants us to listen to Him. He wants us to know His voice. It blows me away that God wants to be close to His children! So rather than preaching: *"You should know Jesus and have a relationship with Him,"* listen to the young person. In doing so, you model knowing Him as a friend and Savior.

EMPATHIZE

When you acknowledge their struggle, pain, and confusion, you strengthen the relationship. Something as simple as *"I am so sorry; that has to be hard"* builds trust. And let me tell you, if you do not do these two things—listen and empathize—you will not get the opportunity to share Jesus because they will turn and run from you before you get there. When they share their situation with you, look them in the eye and say, *"Hey, I'm so sorry you're going through that."*

Even if you don't get them, even if you don't understand what they are experiencing, even if you radically disagree with their ideals, you can be intentionally kind to them and empathize with their pain. Remember that Jesus loves them. And the issues they're struggling with are secondary. If (hopefully when) they reconcile with Jesus, those issues will be resolved in their relationship with Him.

This can also be a time when you share your vulnerabilities. If the young person confesses their battle with loneliness or depression, and you've fought the same battles, your openness to share from your own experience can open the door to further conversation with you. When they know you understand what they're going through, they are more likely to trust you and open up even more.

You have to meet them in their crisis to talk to them about Christ because they won't take the time otherwise. If you flag them down and you give them two choices: 1) Let's talk about your pain, or 2) Let's talk about theological issues, they're going to go to the pain every time. They're going to talk about what they're struggling with. So, that's really where you start. The doorway is through the real-life concerns, challenges, and situations, but handled correctly that doorway can lead to the deeply spiritual.

On our chat line at Groundwire, many times the coach turns the conversation around and says, *"Can I tell you what I did when I needed hope?"* They share their personal story and oftentimes results in the caller coming to Christ.

TRANSITION

When a young person starts to open up, there is a stirring going on in their heart. They may begin to bleed emotionally in front of you, listen, empathize, then transition. It is important to turn toward a spiritual conversation, but it can't be abrupt. You don't just tell them Jesus is the answer. Instead of blurting out *"What you need is Jesus,"* you can say, *"Based on what I'm hearing you say, it sounds like what you're looking for is Jesus."* There is a notable difference between declaring *"You need Jesus"* and gently saying *"You know, as you're sharing your story with me, what I hear is there's a hole in your heart. And I think what you're really searching for is God. Can we talk about that?"* One will shut them down; the other will light them up.

How we transition is so important. In this, let me just encourage you to look closely at yourself and how you offer grace and truth. There are different Baby Boomer and Gen X personalities that tend to gravitate toward either end of this. One end says, *"I'm so empathetic and I care so much, but I don't know how to transition, so I never get to share."*

I've talked to so many people who find it difficult to move

beyond the transition in their conversations with hurting young people. Usually they're really kindhearted, deeply spiritual people, oftentimes women, whose heart is broken when they hear the young person's story, and they get stuck there. They are so compassionate they stay on the upper register. These tender hearts listen and empathize, but they don't transition. So they never get to share Jesus.

At the other end of the spectrum are those, usually men, who tend to speak truth with gusto. In other words, all they want to do is share. They're eager to talk and give truth, skipping directly to what the young person should do. All of us could use more practice in this area of transition, whether we tend toward compassion and grace or gravitate toward the bottom line of making a choice.

We need to first listen with compassion, identify with their pain, and tenderly let them know we understand. Then we suggest Jesus is the answer.

If you listen, empathize, and transition, it gives you the opportunity to share, and that's when you get to share the truth that will make all the difference in their young lives.

SHARE

The connection you've made is a good start. But don't just leave it on the surface. Show them how Jesus is relevant. He becomes relevant the moment He intersects their pain point, whether it's a broken heart, loneliness, lack of purpose, or anxiety. Share how He's the only one who is always with you and will never leave you. Jesus becomes personally relevant when the young person desperate for purpose realizes He intentionally created them, that He knows what's inside of them, can draw the best out of them, and will never leave or abandon them.

This is the time to let them know how Jesus changes everything, and it starts when they understand and respond to His offer of grace, forgiveness, and salvation. Jesus is the giver of hope, life, peace, joy, comfort. He is the answer to every meaningful question they are asking, so don't be afraid to share. Share the love, mercy, compassion, and kindness of Jesus as opposed to judgment.

You can say something as simple as:

"I know your heart is broken, but I want you to know that Jesus wants to heal your heart."

"I know it seems that life will never get better, but I promise you, God has a great plan for you. Life may not be perfect, but He will never leave you."

Take that next step and tell them that God sent Jesus to pay the price for their sin so that He could have a relationship with Him, and anyone who places their trust in Jesus receives forgiveness, eternal life, is adopted as a child of God, and gains the Holy Spirit. All of the promises God offers are available to those who have accepted His gift of salvation and are walking in relationship with Him.

Don't assume they believe this already or even know it. Don't make the mistake of trusting that because they come from a good family or even have attended church growing up that they understand how to have an intimate, personal relationship with Jesus.

Use the relational equity that you have built to introduce them to your best Friend and the One who wants to be theirs as well. (See Rescue Plan in Chapter 10 and on page 189 for more help on how to share the gospel.)

If the young person seems resistant, you can practice a gentle tactic that works especially well. I call it "talking over their shoulder." State your message in third person, instead of pushing the truth at them. Don't directly tell them what to do or spout to their face what they need; instead, tell them what you want them to hear as if you're saying it to someone else. This is what it looks like: *"I've seen so many people looking for the real truth and end up realizing they do believe in God, that He has the answers they've been seeking."* I tell about other situations and individuals, not the person I'm talking with. The message I want them to hear comes through in a non-threatening way.

When the person I'm sharing with becomes combative, I'll say something like, *"I know you think this is preachy, but I just want you to know, I've seen that so many people are finding hope in what I'm sharing with you."* I don't react or get indignant. I don't say, "Well, you're wrong. You need Jesus." I let the truth speak for itself.

I think Paul used this tactic when he spoke to the people of Athens about what they were worshipping. As he walked around their grounds, he found an altar with the inscription: TO AN UNKNOWN GOD. Instead of condemning them or telling them they were wrong, he assures them he's there to help them discover who the unknown God really is. He begins by affirming them, acknowledging how religious they were. He doesn't do this in a belittling or negative way, but connects with them over a common interest. As I read that account in Acts 17:22–23, I picture Paul speaking over their shoulder. He wasn't criticizing or confronting them. He was sharing truth in an indirect way.

And remember, even if they don't soften to our words at the time, the seed of love has been planted. We know God uses some to plant, others to water, and He is the One who tends to the growth of each individual (1 Corinthians 3:6–9).

L.E.T.S. is such an effective non-ambushing tool to help us connect with the younger generations. It works with new friends and with longtime relationships as well. You listen. You empathize. You transition. You share. And you let Jesus draw their hearts to Him.

CHAPTER 7

Radical Assumptions

Since, then, we know what it is to fear the Lord, we try to persuade others. What we are is plain to God, and I hope it is also plain to your conscience (2 Corinthians 5:11).

I WAS WITH a colleague at a restaurant in Chicago when a sweet young woman bussing our table asked, "Is there anything else I can get for you?"

I looked at her and asked, "Hey, how are you? How's your life going? You doing okay?"

"Yeah, I am doing okay."

"Really?" I responded. "Because they say a huge percentage of your generation struggles with anxiety, most of or all of the time."

"Yeah," she admitted. "I guess I fall in that category. I do struggle with anxiety. In fact, if I'm totally honest, my heart is kind of broken."

I looked at her with kindness. "Oh, I'm so sorry. I want you to know there's a God in heaven who understands what you're going through and He wants to help."

You know what she said to me? "Oh, I believe in God. I just

don't believe He can heal my heart. I really don't see how He can help me with my anxiety or my fear. I have to do that on my own."

I've seen evidence of that statement come through in the way many young people live. They believe in God. They just think He's either impotent or He doesn't care. Until this conversation, I'd never had anyone actually articulate it.

"I'm so sorry to hear that," I replied. "And that makes me so sad because I want you to know God's love for you. He hates to see you struggle."

She stood quietly holding the tray of empty cups, so I took it a little bit further. "Actually, I want you to know that God is the one who created you, and only He knows what broke your heart. Therefore, He's the only one who can heal it."

She nodded, indicating she thought that made sense.

"And on top of that, my guess is when you're talking to your therapist, you can't even come up with the words to describe your anxiety. You just know that you feel anxious." I took a step of faith that she had a therapist.

"Yeah, I don't even know how to tell anybody, but I just know what's going on inside of me."

"God created you; He can heal that."

"I want to believe it."

Then I asked if I could pray for her. She nodded and set the tray on our table. With her permission, I held her hand and we prayed.

As soon as we were done, she backed up and rubbed her arms. "Oh! That was awesome! I have goosebumps."

"That's because He's real. What you're sensing is His presence. And He wants you to know His presence all the time."

We didn't get to finish the conversation because she got called away on a restaurant emergency. As my friend and I were standing up to leave, she ran back to our table.

"I really want to finish the conversation, but I don't have time right now. Can you come back another time so we can talk some more?"

"I'm sorry, I'm getting on a plane tomorrow. But you can go to one of our websites." I pointed her to JesusCares.com. "All you need to do is log in to chat with one of our volunteers. Tell them 'I just had this experience. I sensed God's presence. I want to know that all the time.'"

Two weeks later, she got online, and she gave her life to Christ.

This is the story of one young person who was rescued for eternity because God allowed me to guide her into a conversation about faith.

Depending on how much time you've spent with Millennials or Gen Z lately, you might be surprised at what I'm going to share with you in this chapter. We each have our preconceived ideas about the younger generations based on what we see or hear—from young people directly or from the buzz about them on the news or from the stories we hear on the street. There's no denying that contemporary culture belittles Christian values, lumping all believers into a category of ignorant phobics who hate anyone who doesn't believe the way they do. In addition, modern television and cinema portray all young people as atheist and liberal, following their "own truth," averse to associating with narrow-minded Jesus followers. Christians have become the unspoken enemy, and what we represent—God, truth, conviction, prayer—appear to be archaic beliefs in today's society. It seems logical to assume everyone under the age of 50 follows these widespread beliefs.

But we would be wrong. So very wrong.

Young people today are more complex than they might seem on the surface. They don't follow rules or leaders ignorantly. They won't adhere to customs or traditions unless they see the value. Unlike generations of the past, kids of today aren't as likely to automatically adopt the beliefs of their parents. They are thinking deeply (sometimes skeptically), and they value authenticity. When we were younger, we'd never consider arguing religion with Grandpa. Not so for kids today. They want truth and proof and they're not afraid to admit it.

I'd say these are prime conditions for diving into deep conversations about faith!

After participating in and observing thousands upon thousands of conversations, in person and through the many stories at Groundwire, I've come to realize there are assumptions the older generations have been getting wrong. And because of our misunderstanding, we've missed countless opportunities to interact in life-giving ways with the younger generations. With this new understanding, there are four assumptions that I make to help me have authentic, meaningful, and spiritual conversations with young people every day.

Rather than succumbing to negative assumptions—that kids today don't want to talk with us or to have anything to do with Jesus—these four radical assumptions prove otherwise. Young people deserve more credit than we're giving them. They are more open than we assume. But we need to approach them the right way.

These four assumptions will help guide you into impactful spiritual conversations. Whether you're talking with an employee or coworker, a server or salesclerk or young person from down the street, or one of your own kids or grandkids around the dining room table, consider the difference employing these four assumptions could make.

Four Assumptions

Four assumptions:
- They respond to kindness.
- They will answer questions.
- They believe in God.
- They will let you pray for them.

ASSUMPTION 1: THEY WILL RESPOND TO KINDNESS.

This sounds so basic, but I've already stated the sad fact Christians don't have a reputation of being loving or joyful. We also aren't seen as kind. Generally speaking, as Christians we need to step up our game. We need to be kind. You may have heard this before, but servers at restaurants typically say Christians are the worst tippers and are some of the most self-absorbed and rude patrons on Sunday afternoons. Many don't like working Sundays because of the church crowd. It should not be that way.

What do young people think when they see us frowning, grumbling, complaining, criticizing? We don't stand a chance of reaching them if we exhibit impatience or frustration with them. And we most definitely knock out our chances of sharing Jesus with them if we jump into telling them what we think about how wrong they are. They will not respond to judgment.

They do, however, respond to kindness. This is the way God designed it. Rather than enforcing judgment or spewing condemnation, our loving Father reaches out to the lost generations through His kindness. The apostle Paul wrote to the Romans to explain that it's God's kindness that leads us to repentance. *"Or do you show contempt for the riches of his kindness, forbearance and patience, not realizing that God's kindness is intended to lead you to repentance"* (Romans 2:4)?

Think about that. Let it sink in.

This concept is so countercultural to us as Christians. If you grew up in the church, you undoubtedly have heard a sermon teaching that repentance means to turn 180 degrees, to go in the opposite direction. Romans 2:4 actually says that Jesus' kindness is what makes people say to Jesus, I want to be like you. It is His kindness that makes people want to turn in the other direction.

Too often, as Christians we place so much emphasis on the turning that we miss the heart of where change begins. We focus on the behavior, wanting people to repent so their behavior will be more like ours. Somehow we've perched ourselves on our own truth. *"My truth is better than your truth,"* we announce. *"So you'll want to be like me. Shape up and get it right."*

People all around us are beaten down with biblical truths that are weaponized. How this must make Jesus weep. Jesus didn't beat his followers into being like Him; He loved them into it. And He still does that today. Scripture says that because of His kindness and compassion, people will want to change their behavior. God draws us to Him with the promise of forgiveness and cleansing us from unrighteousness (1 John 1:9). It is His kindness that leads us to repentance.

So how do we show this kind of kindness? We lead with words of affirmation, interest, and kind facial expressions. We ask questions. We choose to listen and not preach. We overlook the offensive words and wild outfit, and we keep giving loving attention, no matter how hard they try to push us away with their resistance. We keep our negative opinions to ourselves, refusing to be baited into senseless arguments designed to get us off track. And we show sincere concern, empathizing with their pain, encouraging them, and following up with compassion.

When you express kindness, when you take the time to wait patiently and consistently show compassion, they'll stick around. Believe me, a smile goes a long way.

ASSUMPTION 2: THEY WILL ANSWER QUESTIONS.

The second assumption is that they will answer questions.

Culture has developed this mindset that kids want to be left alone. I don't agree. They like it when people show interest in them. They will answer questions if they feel comfortable and safe with the person asking.

I think sometimes we don't ask questions because we're afraid of how they might answer. That's a fear we need to get over, because their answers can hint at what's going on inside of them. As we prepare ourselves to respond kindly to however they answer, we step out in faith and ask legitimate questions that show sincere interest.

As we've already discussed, they can see through phoniness. But they will respond honestly to an authentic question if they see you're being real, that your interest and concern are real. To be sure, if you ask questions with a combative attitude, you'll get nowhere. It has to come from a smile that has already convinced your companion you really care.

This assumption applies to strangers as well as young people we know well. They will answer questions. Do you know that one of the challenges we have with kids in our circle of influence is we don't ask them enough questions? We tend to tell them long stories about our past that oftentimes don't interest them, or we try to bring light with our wisdom. This reveals how much we actually don't know about them. They do not want to be entertained and they do not want to be taught. They want to be heard. So don't dominate the conversation; ask great questions.

Look them in the eye and say, *"Hey, how you doing?"* From that first question, you can gauge if they're willing to talk to you. You can start with generic questions like, *"Tell me something interesting about yourself."* Or probe a little deeper. *"Tell me about your faith background."* Ask a question and then be quiet. They will respond to questions. If you take time to ask specific questions and then remain patient in listening to them, that earns you the right to speak into their life. Remember what's going on in their life so you can ask more directed questions the next time you see them. *"How are you doing with your project?" "How's your family?"* These kids want to be seen and known. And if they're heard, they'll listen to you in return.

If they're heard, they'll listen.

ASSUMPTION 3: THEY BELIEVE IN GOD.

When I do training with pastors, they're very surprised to see the statistics stating the average young person believes in God, even if they don't attend church or exhibit Christian convictions. You might find this surprising as well. It's certainly not the popular message being promoted today. As older adults, many of us have an inherent fear that we're going to offend, even anger, or dive into a heated debate with young people if we begin a conversation about God.

Let me explain; this is foundational. As we covered in Chapter 2, there are monotheists in the world and there are atheists, but the middle group includes the majority of young people in our nation, especially those in their teens, twenties, and thirties—the Millennials and Gen Z.

As we looked at earlier, the Urban Dictionary defines an apatheist as a young person who believes in God but ignores Him. The majority of young people in our nation believe in God. The younger generations haven't rejected God. They just ignore Him altogether. So you are not offending them when you start talking to them about a loving God who's compassionate. They believe He's there, albeit distant and irrelevant.

Statistics show 71% of Millennials and 64% of Gen Z believe in God.[24] Now, the uniqueness of that statistic is they might not believe in the God that we believe in, but they believe in a God. They believe in the possibility of a higher power or something, someone, bigger than they are. They look at Creation and listen to their forebearers claiming it happened without a Creator, and they are beginning to believe that the logic behind that theory is wrong. The younger generations, especially Gen Z, seem to have better logic centers than most Millennials. They look at how Millennials have tried to convince them and they say, *"That just makes no sense."* They don't necessarily want to believe it, but they don't see how to avoid it. Too many unanswered questions cause them to take on an attitude of apathy. That way, they aren't required to take a stand.

24. Barna Group. (2023, August 16). "Atheism doubles among generation Z." https://www.barna.com/research/atheism-doubles-among-generation-z/

Their attitude is, *"I believe in God. He just doesn't mean anything to me."* We don't need to convince them He's real. Statistics say they know that already. We need to remind them that He's relevant. He becomes relevant when He interacts with their pain points. He becomes relevant when He helps them understand they're never alone. And He becomes relevant when they understand He created them on purpose and He knows the best direction for their life that brings peace, joy, and meaning.

Yes, God has holy standards, but if you start with His compassion and His love and His care, you will have the ability to tell the whole story that comes with it. They need to know they were created to walk in intimate relationship with their Creator, to know their purpose, that He answers every question they're asking, and He provides every need they're searching for. We can help the younger generations understand how relevant God is and what a difference a relationship with Him truly makes in their life.

ASSUMPTION 4: THEY WILL LET YOU PRAY FOR THEM.

Once you've had an open and honest conversation, you've shown kindness and asked questions, listening attentively to their answers, they are surprisingly open to letting you pray for them.

When I ask a young person if I can pray for them, around 80% of the time they will say yes. I'll casually say, "Hey, could I pray for you?" and they'll very often respond with "Yes, you can." Fifteen to twenty percent will say, "Yes, absolutely you can pray for me, but not here. Like when you're driving on the way home, then you can pray for me." They're embarrassed by the process of being prayed for in public.

But very rarely do I have anybody say, "No. Don't pray for me." I've had this happen only perhaps 1% of the time. I find this realization absolutely remarkable. Young people want to know they're cared about, and the fact they are open to being prayed for indicates an openness to the power of a living God.

And here's the deal... prayer has real effects. We are inviting a guest with us into the presence of a living, powerful, interactive God. We're not spouting useless words; we are entering into intercessory prayer on the behalf of this special young person God has allowed us to connect with. We know confidently that God hears our prayers, and He answers in mysterious and divine ways. One prayer with a willing young adult can make a world of difference in their life.

It is essential we all embrace these four assumptions and learn how to lead others into meaningful conversations so we can reach, contend for, the next generations. As more of us choose to live by these four assumptions, we will begin to see way more meaningful conversations happening. More young people will open their hearts to a life with Jesus. We're not forcing anything on them. We're acting on four radical assumptions that make sharing our faith so much simpler.

Let me help put you at ease here. We don't always need to know exactly what to say. Sometimes the Holy Spirit gives us that little prompt of what to say. In those times, like I did with the sweet busser in Chicago, just take a step and listen to the Lord. He knows what will capture their attention and He will lead you.

Remember, others will respond to kindness, whether at work, at home, wherever you may be. If you want your faith to impact others, they have to see you as a kind individual who cares about them. As you enter into a conversation with a young person, keep in mind they will answer questions. It's very meaningful to them when you take the time to have a sincere conversation, asking personal questions and listening attentively. Most young people believe in God, so you're not going to put them off by bringing Him up. And then you've prepared the way to ask, *"Hey, can I pray for you?"* These four assumptions have altered the way I interact with young people, and I can assure you—it works.

CHAPTER 8

Purposeful Prompts

The Lord appeared to us in the past, saying: "I have loved you with an everlasting love; I have drawn you with unfailing kindness" (Jeremiah 31:3).

How is it possible I am 27-years-old and no one has ever told me God loves me?"

I was shocked. This young man's statement rang in my ears and grieved my heart. Twenty-seven years old, living in "One Nation Under God" with a church on every corner and a Christian radio station on every dial, and no one had ever told him that God loved him. He had no idea God has a plan for his life or that God is the answer to every meaningful question he would ever ask. The young man went on to tell me he grew up in church. He seemed to remember he'd been told he was disappointing to God. He hadn't been taught that God cared about him on a personal level. No one had ever shared that God loved this young man so much He made a way to spend eternity with him. So the very first time he heard about God's love and His plan of salvation, he jumped in with both feet.

That conversation was one of the most enjoyable and memorable I have had so far. I was quick to give God praise and quick to share this young man's story with others.

A couple of days later, I revisited the line that kept echoing in my mind: "How is it possible I am 27-years-old and no one has ever told me God loves me?" I wondered how many people just like this young man had never heard the affirming words that would bring them toward peace and one step closer to Jesus. How many young people are stuck in a place of spiritual darkness because they have not been introduced to the One who brings light?

Jesus spread His light wherever He went, holding out His hand as an invitation to everyone trapped in the Enemy's darkness. And His light continues to shine and call into the darkness through the generations. He said, *"I am the light of the world. Whoever follows me will never walk in darkness, but will have the light of life"* (John 8:12).

> Shining His light into their darkness can be as simple as initiating meaningful spiritual conversations with sincere interest and a loving listening ear.

Jesus promises unending light. Yet, if they're never told, how will they know? The truth is, we have entire generations stumbling through spiritual darkness, not knowing the Light of the World is waiting open-armed for them to come to Him. They are being held captive by an empty darkness that is keeping them separate from eternal hope. Shedding His light into their darkness can be as simple as initiating meaningful spiritual conversations with sincere interest and a loving listening ear.

Everyday Dialogue

As you think about those in your circle—kids, grandkids, friends, coworkers—consider how to move them toward God's love. This can happen quite naturally as you pursue regular, meaningful conversations. As you begin applying the principles in this book, and you start listening more attentively to God's whispers, you will discover you're starting to have meaningful spiritual conversations every day.

The more you practice and step out in faith with initiating dialogue, you'll find you're able to talk more comfortably about the Lord Jesus and your personal relationship with Christ in compelling and authentic ways. You will also find yourself easing into discussions about other people's personal relationship with Him. These conversations don't come from a place of preaching heaven and hell, make a decision, turn or burn, but in talking about the beauty of relationship that God offers and the gratitude that you have for yours.

We all want to lead young people in the right direction, and for the greatest purpose of all—to a personal relationship with Jesus. We are learning how to lead people to Jesus through meaningful spiritual conversations, and this can happen within your own home and family, as well as with people you meet in restaurants, on the airplane, on golf courses, pickle ball courts, at social events, waiting in long lines, wherever you find yourself with the time and opportunity to talk for a while. After you've followed the steps to engage the young person in dialogue, expressed interest and compassion, and you realize this young soul seems willing to go deeper, now is the time to ask questions to steer toward a personally spiritual discussion.

I understand this can be easier said than done. The uncertainty of what to say has paralyzed many well-intentioned people, preventing meaningful spiritual conversations from happening. It helps to have a purposeful guideline to lean on, rather than trying to come up with what to say every time.

Prompt Spiritual Discussion

Quite regularly, I rely on the following three questions to start spiritual conversations. These points serve as invaluable prompts to engage in meaningful dialogue wherever you are and with whatever person God brings across your path.

1. What brings you hope?
2. Has anyone ever shared with you how you can be close to God?
3. What do you think Jesus sees when He looks at you?

If you ask these questions in a relational, conversational way, they will lead to meaningful discussions that open the doorway into another person's spiritual well-being.

> Questions to prompt spiritual conversation:
> - What brings you hope?
> - Has anyone ever shared with you how you can be close to God?
> - What do you think Jesus sees when He looks at you?

QUESTION 1: WHAT BRINGS YOU HOPE?

When a young person reveals they are struggling with anxiety, fear, relationally, etc., you can ask, *"Where do you go to find hope?"*

They typically don't have a great answer.

You can follow up with, *"Could I share where I go when I need hope and perspective?"* The door opens, and you can share how Jesus brings you peace, courage, and hope and how He offers eternal solutions as well.

Even if they have something that brings them hope, a lot of times it's fluff. Meditation, music, or getting in sync with the earth's vibrations or whatever. I listen and respond with something like, *"That's great. But I just want you to know that God wants to walk with you through this."* This allows you to take the conversation a little bit deeper.

QUESTION 2: HAS ANYONE EVER SHARED WITH YOU HOW YOU CAN BE CLOSE TO GOD?

In the last couple of years, I have discovered something that helps me have very meaningful conversations with many who are unchurched. They want to be close to God. You might not be able to tell based on their behaviors and conversations, but internally, something within them is crying out to know Him and to walk with the God of the universe.

When in a conversation, I often suggest, "I get the sense you want to be close to God." After a nod or agreement, I ask the question: "Has anyone ever told you how you can be really close with Him every day?" The answer is typically "No."

That opens the door for me to ask, "Would you mind if I share that with you?" Do you know that whenever I've asked that question, I've never been turned down?

Then I offer them the gospel and dive into the Rescue Plan.

"Let me tell you how. You're loved by the God who created all of this, and He created you. And He wants to be close to you too. That's what blows me away. Not that I want to be close to Him, but that He wants to be close to me… and He wants to be close to you, too. God loves you and wants to walk with you through life, to comfort you through challenges, and to help you discover your unique purpose. Unfortunately, there is a huge divide between you and God.

"Picture this. Even though God created you intentionally and loves you deeply, there is a deep divide between you and Him. It is almost as if He is on the other side of a huge gorge. You can see Him and you want to get to Him, but you can't. He wants you to be close, but the deep pit is a problem.

"Do you know what caused that gap?"

Almost always the young person responds with "No," opening the door to share the Rescue Plan with them (more on this in the next chapter).

Do not fall for the mask they're hiding behind. Do not buy the hardness. Do not buy the media lies that say they are not interested, because as I've already stated, young people are more open to the gospel right now than they've ever been. When the world is messed up, young people are more open to the gospel because it offers hope.

QUESTION 3: WHAT DO YOU THINK JESUS SEES WHEN HE LOOKS AT YOU?

I typically get two answers to that one: 1) *"He doesn't see me. I think He's ignoring me. I'm invisible,"* or 2) *"I don't think He likes what He sees."* Either response gives a great opportunity for love and compassion to step into that conversation with them. *"Let me tell you what God sees when He looks at you. He adores you, and He has great plans for you."* Most of the time, the young person is surprised to hear how God sees them. With wounded self-esteem and confused identity about their own purpose and value, they are more likely to see God as disapproving and distant. They don't expect God to have such a personal interest in their lives. When they realize He sees them in such an accepting, loving way, their hearts open to hear more.

I use these three questions to get people into spiritual conversations all the time. These important prompts have proven to spark many eye-opening and life-giving conversations. As I've said frequently, asking questions and listening attentively can open the door to a young person's heart, allowing you the opportunity to lead them closer to Jesus with every conversation.

Several years ago I did a training at a church on how to have meaningful spiritual conversations. For that seminar, I focused on the role of parents and grandparents in reaching the next generations for Jesus.

Six months later, I heard from a grandmother who had attended my training session. She shared, "I have a 16-year-old grandson, and I've been wanting to have meaningful conversations with him about spiritual things, but every time I tried he got kind of riled up. He pushed away and said he didn't want to have those conversations.

"So, after your training session, I decided to try asking more meaningful questions. We were all together at a family meal, and I just said, 'What's one word that everybody would use to describe their spiritual life?' My granddaughter piped up with 'Strong! Meaningful!' My grandson said 'Non-existent.'"

The grandma went on to share how later she asked her grandson, "You know, I'm interested to hear more about your answer to my question at the dinner table, if you would like to share more."

He finally opened up a little. "Yeah, I don't even know what I believe. It just seems fake to me. I mean, I believe there's a God. I just don't know what that looks like."

The wise grandmother listened patiently before she responded.

Then she said, "I'm going to begin to pray for you that you would really be guided. That God will reveal Himself to you and that you'd really begin to understand what that looks like."

She told me that about a month later, she followed up on their conversation with a text. She just wrote, "Hey, I was praying for you today."

Her grandson replied, "Thank you! I'm going to youth group with a friend."

Grandma continued to pray and follow-up with texts. One day her grandson texted her how "youth group was really, really cool." Eventually, he ended up giving his life to Christ and getting baptized in that church. And it all started when one brave grandma asked a meaningful question around the dinner table.

CHAPTER 9

When They Walk Away

"What do you think? If a man owns a hundred sheep, and one of them wanders away, will he not leave the ninety-nine on the hills and go to look for the one that wandered off? And if he finds it, truly I tell you, he is happier about that one sheep than about the ninety-nine that did not wander off. In the same way your Father in heaven is not willing that any of these little ones should perish" (Matthew 18:12-14).

THIS BOOK is about capturing the Millennials and Gen Z with the gospel message. But how do we capture young people who already know the gospel message and have walked away from it?

Many of the topics we have covered in earlier chapters resonate with young people who have never been a part of a church. When we ask them, *"Where do you go for hope?"* and then follow up with stories of going to God, it is often an eye-opening experience for them. They've never known about the intimate interest of a loving God. But if we try to tell our kids who have walked away where we go for hope… they already know. They were raised with that

111

example. They know their Christian parents go to God for hope. So how do we reach them?

A troubled mom reached out to me recently for help. Her three Millennials have walked away from their faith and she doesn't know how to help them find their way back. As kids, they did all the church, Sunday School, youth group stuff. Even at home, they were raised with daily Bible readings, regular prayer, and godly teaching. I could hear the desperation in this mom's voice as she asked me for help.

> They might not be as far away as you think.

"Sean, I just don't know what to do. My kids grew up knowing all about God. But as they got into their young adult years, they were swayed by the culture and now they're believing all the Enemy's lies. They've walked away from the church and it's very difficult to know what to do. Please help me. I am desperate."

Tragically, this is an all-too-common situation in our post-Christian culture. For several years, even decades, we've been watching high schoolers leave the church after graduation. Liberal education at universities and social pressure from unbelieving peers in all kinds of liberal circles have proven to be powerful influences. In trying to find their own way, many church-raised young people are searching for truth in unreliable places, and I can tell you their newly embraced mindsets aren't founded on anything solid.

All this points to what I told this hurting mom.

"What I see is that prodigals oftentimes reject institutionalized religion or traditional church. They even reject our faith as parents or grandparents. But many of them don't reject Jesus."

I say this to encourage a lot of hurting parents who are watching their kids take the dark road away from the faith they knew at home. As you're watching the gate for them to return, consider this: They might not be as far away as you think.

A young man who had been raised in a Christian home logged on to our website and he said, "I'm an atheist, but I'm starting to wonder if there really is a God. What do I do now?"

He couldn't go to Mom and Dad because he had claimed to be an atheist just to put up a barrier between himself and his parents.

The online coach replied, "You know what, I get the feeling you're not really an atheist. You know that there's a God. You've just been running from Him." The barrier started to come down and the volunteer was able to gently lead the young man back into a relationship with Jesus and his mom and dad.

I talk to so many older adults who are worried because their Millennial or Gen Z kids don't want to go to church anymore. These concerned parents are convinced their sons and daughters have rejected their faith. But I've seen over the years that many of them haven't rejected their beliefs entirely. Many leave the church because they don't like the structure or attitudes they see within organized religion, so they become an apatheist as we covered in Chapter 2, trying to ignore what they know deep inside. I know people who haven't been in church and haven't read the Bible in twenty years who will defend their faith against an atheist. Many prodigals won't come out and tell their parents directly they're no longer a Christian because they still hold that belief in the back of their mind.

However, I recognize this isn't the case for everyone. Some teens and young adults have taken deliberate steps away from their faith, radically embracing other religions or philosophies, and it breaks a parent's heart. But be encouraged today. Jesus Himself told us the parable about the loving shepherd who went out to rescue the one lost sheep. His message holds true for us as parents of prodigals. Jesus sees every single one of our kids who has wandered away. Not a single one is lost from His sight. And He fully intends for them to be captured and returned—one at a time—with His love.

Either way, whether they are only rebelling against church traditions or if they are adopting contrary beliefs, when our kids pull away, it hurts us. Any parent or grandparent of a prodigal understands the anguish of that pain and fear for our deceived loved ones.

We're all familiar with the story of the prodigal son. Jesus told this story to the Pharisees and the teachers of the law after they complained about how He hung around with sinners. His heart for broken people shines through as He describes the scene of the son returning home. *"But while he was still a long way off, his father saw him and was filled with compassion for him; he ran to his son, threw his arms around him and kissed him"* (Luke 15:20). That's how Jesus feels about our children who have walked away. He longs for them to return home to their childlike faith and foundation in Him as much as we do.

Yet, just as the rebellious son's dad had to watch his son walk away, the young man's money bags full of his earthly inheritance, sometimes we find ourselves needing to do the same thing. It grieves us to watch them walk away, but there comes a time when they have to make their own decisions and mistakes.

To bring some comfort to aching hearts of many parents and grandparents, I want to remind you that those who walk away from church, their faith—or our faith—everything we tried so hard to teach them, are still in God's sights. He sees them and longs for them to return home. Better than anyone else, Jesus understands the lies of the tempter. He stood against those lies in the wilderness and died for the results of the Enemy's lies on the cross. Jesus knows the battle is real, and He intends for us to carry our cross with Him and engage in combat alongside Him. The calling to contend for a generation isn't only for the ones who have never heard about the truth found in Jesus. It also includes fighting for those who have known and have walked away.

Why They're Pulling Away

We've already covered some of the reasons so many kids are leaving the church. They don't feel authentic love there. They feel judged. They've experienced the two-sided nature of too many regular churchgoers, and they've had enough. Their questions aren't being addressed, mainly because they don't feel safe to ask. So they go outside the church in search of answers.

Many parents feel they are responsible for their children walking away. They beat themselves up, convinced their shortcomings are the reason their prodigal has turned their back on their faith: They didn't pray enough, they lost their temper too many times, they couldn't get a handle on their addiction. They failed to teach the right lessons or didn't teach them well enough. They didn't give their kids enough attention, or they indulged them by giving them too much. Some believe the divorce was the tipping point. Whatever the personal faults they see, parents of prodigals feel the hopeless weight of blame on their shoulders. I've spoken with so many parents who carry the heavy burden of feeling entirely responsible for the choices their child has made. In their eyes, these hurting parents firmly and painfully believe they are the reason their kids have run away.

Even the most devout, mature Christian parent will make mistakes. That doesn't imply we are hypocrites; it confirms we are human. We believe what we say, but we haven't always been the best example. Sometimes we do and say things we wish we hadn't. I understand how difficult this can be for parents of prodigals. But listen; all kids see the faults and failures of their parents. In fact, our kids see more than most of us realize. They know we are not perfect. This fact does not make us responsible for the choices they make. Truly, many factors contribute to a child's rebellion, and only God can see them clearly.

Some reasons for a young person to turn away from their childhood faith come from a more personal place within them, whether they can admit it or not. Young people may pull away from church and a godly family because of the holiness represented there. They watch their friends living loose and free, and they don't want to be bound to godly standards, so they ditch the whole thing. They'd rather live inside rules of their own making than submit to God's righteous standards. Dwelling on all the supposed "don't do this and don't do that," they convince themselves the problem is the strict way of living, not their own rebellion.

Sometimes Millennials and Gen Z pull away from God because of what He expects. They want to be their own decision maker, in charge of their own plans for their lives. To surrender to God means laying down their own desires, and too many young people don't want to do that. In a world that worships personal happiness above anyone else's, it's counterculture to deny ourselves, much less choose to surrender our will to God. God expects loyalty, self-sacrifice, humility, and obedience—traits our culture resists.

Sadly, some young people pull away from God and the church because of their own shame. They may have tried to follow Jesus but stumbled and fell into temptation of one kind or another—a purity ring that lost its purpose, a vow to abstain from pornography that the internet overpowered, the inability to say no to alcohol or drugs. Unable to shake the guilt and shame, these hurting young people allow failure to lead them further away from a forgiving God. They follow the same mindset as Adam and Eve, who hid from God in their shame.

While They are Gone

As we know, there is no formula here. No "do these three things and your kids will come running home." But there are principles that we can apply to help keep the door open, making their return more likely.

One principle I've found most effective comes from Paul's letter to the Christians in Thessalonica, as he encouraged them to grow in their faith. Note one of the first things he says, *"... as apostles of Christ we could have asserted our authority"* (1 Thessalonians 2:6). As parents or leaders of prodigals, we are often inclined to use our authority to try to get them to do what we think they should do. With good intentions, we demand they attend church with us when they're home for a holiday or we insist they participate in family prayer like they used to as a child. But in most of these instances, exercising our authority over them only serves to drive them further away.

The more important message from Paul comes next. *"Just as a nursing mother cares for her children, so we cared for you. Because we loved you so much, we were delighted to share with you not only the gospel of God but our lives as well"* (vv. 7–8). Paul wasn't a traveling preacher who dropped commands from the pulpit before riding off to the next town. Paul and Timothy shared their lives with the church, happily. They were gentle, kind, like a caring mother.

Kids who have walked away don't always see this gentleness and kindness, regrettably not in their home or in the church. We can change this today. Rather than retreating from our kids who have walked away, we can follow Paul's example by sharing our lives with them.

Look for ways to be involved in their lives instead of expecting them to take part in your interests. Go where they are and pay attention to what matters to them. Be gentle in your interactions with them, not accusing or demanding. Express genuine care, asking questions about their lives, offering encouragement and empathy. In this way, you are revealing the gospel of Jesus in the sharing of your life with them.

I understand this isn't always the easiest thing to do. Angry prodigals have a way of casting darts into a vulnerable parent's heart, but we can trust the Holy Spirit to comfort us as we intentionally invest in the lives of our kids. For them to see Jesus in us, they need to see us being kind, gentle, and present.

A little later in Paul's letter, he writes to the Thessalonians, *"For you know that we dealt with each of you as a father deals with his own children, encouraging, comforting and urging you to live lives worthy of God, who calls you into his kingdom and glory"* (vv. 11–12).

I love these three ways Paul says he was dealing with the church: encouraging, comforting, and urging. He is coaching us how to approach our prodigals. Rather than preaching or scolding, Paul takes on the role of a dad. Think of a wise, loving father as he deals with his unruly children. He encourages, comforts, and urges them on to repentance and a better life.

Too often, young people only hear us begging, pleading, reprimanding, heaping loads of unsolicited advice they don't want to hear. They feel judged, condemned, and at some point along the way they stop listening. The message they're receiving is that we're asking them to be a certain way or to adopt our lifestyle. And they start to put up walls.

In contrast, if we focus on encouraging and comforting them when they struggle, our urging will be better received. Sometimes we just need to come along and express our belief in them. Young people have massive doubts about whether or not they can be a good person. They worry: Can I overcome my addiction? Can I make myself do what's necessary for a happy life? Can I pick someone better than a loser to spend my life with? They are overwhelmed with self-doubt. We can either contribute to that negative voice or combat it with encouragement.

They don't need us harping at them when they're already feeling down. Don't let your words join the negative voice inside their heads. Kids have told me they've heard comments like these from adults in their lives: *"You would be so pretty if it wasn't for your tattoos." "How are you ever going to find a spouse if you can't hold down a job?" "Who's going to want to be with you if you're so broken?"* These are horrible things to say to young people who are already questioning their own worth. When they fail, the last thing they need is for us to heap more condemnation on them.

Instead, offer encouragement and comfort, like Paul did. They need to hear us say, *"You can do it,"* and know that we honestly believe it. When they're facing a tough situation, guide them with *"You've got this. God's with you. He'll help you through it."* Come alongside them and put your arm around them and say, *"It's going to be okay. You're going to learn from this."* If they lose a job, we have an opportunity to encourage them when they're doubting themselves. When somebody breaks up with them, we can comfort them. In times of loss and uncertainty, we assure them everything is going to be okay.

After we have been encouraging and comforting, we earn the right to speak into their life more intentionally, but not before. They must first feel encouraged, comforted, and safe with us before we can urge them to reconsider Jesus.

> They must first feel encouraged, comforted, and safe with us before we can urge them to reconsider Jesus.

Teachable not Preachable Moments

I've had parents ask me if they should try to talk to their prodigals about God or to not go there. "Do we just leave it in God's hands?" they ask. Of course, there are certain acts of God that only He can do. Only He can soften a hardened heart. Yet God has called us to teach the younger generations (Titus 2:3–5). I encourage each of us to look for opportunities to disciple, even if our prodigals don't recognize that's what we're doing. You can still enter into meaningful spiritual conversations with those who have walked away. Many of the principles I share in this book apply, but they have to be done in the right timing and with the right mindset.

Kids who have walked away think all you care about is what you believe. If you start telling them about something God has done in your life or a new faith lesson you've learned, they feel like they're being preached at, even though that's not your intention. There's a difference between a preachable moment and a teachable moment. A preachable moment is when a parent or someone in authority speaks with the attitude, *"I'm going to say it and if you don't respond the first time, I'm going to say it again louder and I'm going to feel justified."* But the prodigal is not going to hear it.

A teachable moment happens as you wait for that chink in the armor, for that door to crack open, and you know you can whisper into it. And in that moment, because they're ready, you're going to have a meaningful conversation.

Unfortunately, most parents gravitate toward preachable moments because we believe so strongly that *"My truth is better than your truth. So you better listen to me."* Worse, our preachable moments even sound like preaching. Within our circles of Christianity, we have adopted our own lingo. We talk about getting together for "fellowship" and we feel so "blessed" when good things happen. Our Christianese language comes so naturally to us as believers, we don't even realize we're doing it. However, this kind of speech feels fake to young people. Remember how much they value authenticity, as we discussed in Chapter 5. We need to challenge ourselves to be authentic, especially in the teachable moments. It is crucial we speak to our kids with words they can identify with, not Christian lingo that feels strange and phony to them. This switch requires being thoughtful and intentional, considering our words carefully. And it will make all the difference.

Even if you're not preaching, don't try to get them talking about spiritual things too often or they will feel like you are nagging them. They will avoid being around you if they think you're going to try to corner them into another Christian discussion. Nothing sends a kid packing quicker than a sermon.

Instead, be on the lookout for teachable moments. For example, your high school student comes home and you can tell by their demeanor they've had a rough day. You go sit down next to them; they lean into you, and they cry on your shoulder. This is an opportunity to steer the topic into a meaningful conversation. For an older Millennial, you look for times when you can see breaks in the armor. The conversation has turned tender or they have just shared some personally challenging news. Pray for wisdom and discernment to recognize teachable moments, because if you try to force a conversation at the wrong time, it doesn't help. But if you do it at the right time, when there's vulnerability, you can watch teachable moments unfold naturally.

So how do you get them going in that direction?

When you recognize a teachable moment, you can ask, *"Can*

I ask you a question? I just would really love to understand where you are spiritually. Would you be willing to share? And if not, that's okay." There are times that it is going to be counterproductive for you to try to have a conversation with them. And if they give you that hint, drop it. You'll have another chance. I've learned this from one of my daughters.

After she shared with me what she believed, I asked, "Could I share with you what I believe?"

"No. I already know what you believe."

"Okay." I smiled and went back to what I was doing.

She was so shocked that I didn't push it.

The next day on the car ride home, she said, "You know, Dad, that was kind of rude of me yesterday. Let's talk about what you believe." A teachable moment had just opened up.

When your teachable moments open, prayerfully consider what questions to ask and listen for the Holy Spirit to guide you. You might gently ask them what they believe. *"I'd really love to understand. What do you believe about God? What changed? How can I help you and support you?" "How would you describe your spiritual life?"* Depending on how safe or open they feel, you may get an honest response. Don't push. Let it happen in its own time. Other potential questions to ask could be: *"What does your friend group think about the church?"* Or... *"Tell me your thoughts about how you were raised. What would you do differently with your kids as it pertains to faith and religion?"*

The goal is to just get them talking. I've discovered that the more they talk, the more they poke holes in their own philosophy. They don't believe half the stuff they claim to believe.

Another way to press lightly is to say, *"I know you're probably not here yet, and you don't think that God's paying attention to you or He cares about you. But I just want you to know, even though you might not believe it, I do. And I'm going to keep praying for you. I want your joy to return. I want peace to replace your anxiety. You may not yet agree with me, but that doesn't change the fact that I am going to keep loving you, praying for you, and wanting the best for you."*

If the prodigal you're talking with has been hurt by people in the church, as so many have, you can speak into that as well. I've learned that when a Christian mistreats a young person, unchurched or faithful, one of the best things you can do is to apologize for the other Christian's behavior, even if you agree with the Christian. You can say, *"You know what? I am so sorry they hurt you. God loves you and would never push you away."* In this, we do have to be careful because we know Jesus confronts sin, but He does it lovingly and compassionately without shutting doors. We don't want to make light of wrong attitudes or immorality, but when another Christian has been rude, aggressively judgmental, or offensive in their behavior, our apology can help redirect the young person back to Jesus and away from the offender. And when a fellow Christian blatantly sins against another person, causing that individual to stumble in their own faith, we can assuredly tell the victim how wrong that whole situation was and offer our apology on behalf of all that Christ represents. Kids who have been wounded by someone in the church need to be reminded all Christians are not that way, and Jesus most certainly is grieved at the sinful behavior of one of His followers.

As I reflect back on the woman who spouted "Have a blessed day" at the protest rally, I recognize that fakeness in even some parents and grandparents. They represent their faith with that same throw-it-in-your-face fashion, and it amounts to nothing except more hurt and anger. As opposed to the authentic Christians who say sincerely, *"I care about you and I'm praying for you."* When somebody comes online and says Christians are some of the meanest, most hypocritical people, our coaches are trained to respond, *"You're right. And I am so sorry you had to experience that. Jesus loves you and even though He might not agree with everything you think, feel, or do, He would never intentionally hurt you."* Sometimes the young person is so caught off guard it lengthens the conversation, opening the door even wider in a teachable moment.

Today I pray you will be mindful of teaching instead of preaching as you wait for your prodigal to return, offering grace in every interaction, and showing God's love every chance you get.

And while you wait, be sure to pray. God has the ability to soften the hardest heart and open the blindest eyes. Pray that God would reveal their emptiness. Ask God to help them know the truth from the lies and that they would stop defending the lies that have already been exposed. Pray they would be reminded of their convictions and the commitments they have made, and pray they would be reminded of the peace and comfort they once found in Him. Ask God to send them the right friends. And pray for your own heart to be tender and full of grace to receive them when they return.

Be Ready to Welcome Them Home

Every parent or grandparent, aunt or uncle, teacher, coach, or leader who has helplessly watched a Millennial or Gen Z walk away wants the same thing: the prodigal to return. We wait and we watch. We pray and we guard our interactions with them carefully, controlling our tongue, keeping our opinions quiet, showing kindness and love, counting the days or years or decades until they return.

When they do come back home to their faith, that's when our next steps really matter.

Wherever prodigals have been, whatever pig trough they have pulled themselves out of, you can be assured they have experienced the agony of sin. Separation from God holds its own sorrow, and when you add to that all the mess they've been exposed to in the Enemy's camp, most definitely they will have guilt and shame to deal with. The best thing you can do to welcome them home is to shower them with love and acceptance, not judgment. No matter how far away they've been, no matter how much darkness they allowed into their lives, don't hold their mistakes against them. They already know what they did wrong and how much grief it caused you. You don't need to point that out to them. They're already overcome with personal doubts and insecurities. They recognize they have messed up and caused themselves and others pain; there's no need to heap any more their direction. This is the time to stand with a compassionate, gracious, forgiving shoulder for them to cry on, to lean on. In taking that posture, you reflect the unconditional love of our heavenly Father.

Stand beside them as they deal with the consequences of their sin. Now, I'm referring to a prodigal who has returned home *to their faith*, not someone who returns home looking for a free place to land but who has not had a heart change. This is where you must pray for discernment so you don't continue to enable sinful behavior. In those times, I suggest you seek godly counsel and pray for wisdom to make the difficult choices on behalf of your continually rebellious loved one. But when a child who has walked away comes home with a broken and repentant heart, that's when you can embrace them with patient support as they work through their own guilt.

It is good for us to take a moment to back up and look at the bigger picture. A lost soul has been rescued from the Enemy. What does Jesus say about that? He tells us that when the shepherd finds the one lost sheep, he "joyfully" put it on his shoulders and carries it home. Then he calls his friends and neighbors to share the great news that his lost sheep was found and is back home safe and sound. He is ecstatic and wants everyone to know (Luke 15:5–6). This is what every young person who has walked away and then returns needs from us. They need us to welcome them joyfully and help carry their burdens. They need us to accept them proudly, letting everyone in our circle know how happy we are they've returned. What they don't need is for us to recount all the bad choices they've made. The shepherd didn't scold the lost sheep or lock it up in a pen as punishment for walking away. Let's follow that example. No guilt. No shame.

Rejoice instead! I can tell you for sure that's what Jesus is doing. He tells us there is *"rejoicing in heaven"* when a person repents (v. 7). And I see the best way of rejoicing is to celebrate this heavenly return alongside our child who has come home. Pray with them. Worship with them. Grow in faith with them. Rejoice with them. You both have much to be grateful for.

It is true that prodigals can break our hearts. They can cause us great pain and make us question our parenting or grandparenting ability. They can make us question our own faith, ability to hear from God, and our own convictions. But, I want to encourage you—if you have people in your life who are not walking passionately with Jesus as you want them to, do not give up. There will come a moment when their demeanor changes, their wall comes down, and they are going to need you. Your prayers can soften them. Whether or not you see it, your walk with Jesus will intrigue them. Your demeanor will bring them comfort. And, at some point, you will get to welcome them home. Keep your eyes on the horizon. Even today they may be coming to their senses. They might already be on their way.

CHAPTER 10

"Do I Matter?"

For God did not send his Son into the world to condemn the world, but to save the world through him. Whoever believes in him is not condemned, but whoever does not believe stands condemned already because they have not believed in the name of God's one and only Son (John 3:17–18).

A YOUNG LADY named Kayla logged into our chat line and typed three simple words:

"Do I matter?"

I watched with interest as our online volunteer Julie engaged with this young woman. They say Millennials have a twelve second attention span, so our coaches are trained not to type in paragraphs, but in short, leading sentences that create a flow. Following these directions, Julie took Kayla deep pretty quick, beginning with affirmation.

"Absolutely," she typed. "You matter. You matter to me. And I'm sure there are people in your life that you matter to. But most importantly, you matter to God. Has anybody ever told you what God sees when He looks at you?"

Kayla said no.

The coach then told her, "Let me tell you what God sees when He looks at you."

She went on to share bursts of Scripture, reinforcing God's view of Kayla.

"You are the apple of His eye."[25]

"You were created in His image."[26]

"You were fearfully and wonderfully made."[27]

"You are the crown of His Creation."[28]

"You are what is most precious to Him."[29]

"He delights over you with singing."[30]

After sharing these powerful one-liners and others about what God sees when He looks at the young lady who wondered if she even mattered, Julie asked, "How does that make you feel?"

"Amazing."

The chat continued as Julie typed, "Not only that, but I want you to know that God thinks you matter so much He doesn't want to spend eternity without you. He made a way so you could spend eternity with Him. That's how much you matter to Him. Has anybody ever shared how you can spend eternity

---

25. Zechariah 2:8
26. Genesis 1:27
27. Psalm 139:14
28. Psalm 8:5
29. Isaiah 43:4
30. Zephaniah 3:17

in heaven with the God who created you, loves you, and can't imagine eternity without you?"

Kayla responded, "I used to attend church, but I don't think anyone ever told me what it takes to get to heaven."

The online volunteer shared that God loves her. She reinforced to Kayla that God created her for a relationship with Him, but sin has separated her from Him. Julie explained how sin comes with a price that we are each unable to pay, but God paid it by sending Jesus to pay the very high price with His life, through His death and resurrection.

And in that simple way, the desperate young woman heard the gospel.

In our ministry, we call it the Rescue Plan.

Rescue Plan

God has made a way for every young life we encounter to be rescued from sin and death, from a dark eternity without Him. No one knows their desperation better than He does. That's why God's Rescue Plan included sending His own Son to save them. His love compels Him to offer every captured person a way back to safety, back to Him.

Because the younger generations are desperate for a divine rescue, we must be bold and intentional in our steps to bring them to freedom in Christ. We are ambassadors on royal assignment to lead young people out of evil captivity. Paul leads the way with his call to action in 2 Corinthians 5:20: *"We are therefore Christ's ambassadors, as though God were making his appeal through us. We implore you on Christ's behalf: Be reconciled to God."*

Our mission is to help captured Millennials and Gen Z be reconciled to God. That is the ultimate rescue.

The first step in the Rescue Plan is to help the young person understand what they need to be rescued *from*. Talking about God's desire to rescue them connects with the pain point we covered earlier: the ache and suffering Millennials and Gen Z are feeling so intensely, their lack of purpose, loneliness, anxiety, uncertainty of the future. But what they really need to be rescued from is sin and spiritual death, from eternal separation from God.

Getting their attention off the temporary "here and now" is critical. Each one needs to understand that eternity is coming, and that Jesus makes it not only bearable, but will give them reason to celebrate.

They know what separation from God feels like because they're living it.

Eternity without God is excruciating and indescribable—a prison called hell that never ends (Matthew 13:41–42, Matthew 5:22, Matthew 25:41, Mark 9:43, Matthew 25:46). A place of torment and anguish—alone without the presence of the kind Father who loves them so deeply. He paid the price so they could spend eternity with Him if they would only choose to give their lives to Him.

"Jesus gave his life for our sins, just as God our Father planned, in order to rescue us from this evil world in which we live" (Galatians 1:4 NLT).

So many young people, as we've seen, are living in their own trap of hell already, confused by what the world is telling them and what their hearts are longing for. They know what separation from God feels like right now because they're living it, but without Jesus, what awaits them is immeasurably more miserable. Actual hell will be unspeakably more painful and more permanent.

When a young person recognizes and admits the need to be rescued, it sets us up to tell them about the great divide. We show them that according to the Bible, the punishment for sin is spiritual death and eternal separation from God.

"For the wages of sin is death, but the gift of God is eternal life in Christ Jesus our Lord" (Romans 6:23).

Explain to the young person that since each of us has sinned, there is a great divide separating us all from God. We cannot get close to God by trying to be good or by becoming religious. There is nothing in and of ourselves that can undo our past mistakes. Our sin has separated us from a holy God.

Make it clear that unless we accept the truth that Jesus died for us so we can cross that divide, ask Him to forgive us, and turn our lives over to Him, we will spend eternity paying for our sin without the light of Jesus to shine in our darkness.

We can help them understand that everyone has sin in their lives. They're not alone. We all fall short of God's perfect standards, and there's nothing we can do on our own to make up for our past mistakes.

"For all have sinned and fall short of the glory of God, and all are justified freely by his grace through the redemption that came by Christ Jesus. God presented Christ as a sacrifice of atonement, through the shedding of his blood—to be received by faith" (Romans 3:23–25). Jesus came to Earth to pay the death penalty for our sin. He was buried and rose from the dead, which was God's plan all along. Jesus overcame sin and death, something human beings could never do on their own. And He offers more than forgiveness; He offers us eternal life with Him, free from the torment of the Enemy and the darkness that he tries to drag us all into.

"For God so loved the world that he gave his one and only Son, that whoever believes in him shall not perish but have eternal life. For God did not send his Son into the world to condemn the world, but to save the world through him. Whoever believes in him is not condemned, but whoever does not believe stands condemned already because they have not believed in the name of God's one and only Son" (John 3:16–18).

Regardless of what a person may think or say, every human being falls under the curse of a broken world and needs to be rescued by Jesus.

This is where we make it personal for the young person. We give them the opportunity to reach out for Jesus' open hand, and we show them how to do that. Ask them if they admit they are separated from God because of their own sin. Invite them to pray and ask Jesus for forgiveness and to tell Him they want to live their life close to Him.

"If you openly declare that Jesus is Lord and believe in your heart that God raised him from the dead, you will be saved. For it is by believing in your heart that you are made right with God, and it is by openly declaring your faith that you are saved" (Romans 10:9–10 NLT).

Many young people are nervous about praying, unsure of what to say. Assure them Jesus is their friend, and that He doesn't condemn His own children. He loves us each, just as we are. Oftentimes it helps to gently guide the person in prayer by having them repeat after you.

Please note that a salvation prayer is not what saves. It is not magic. When I suggest a prayer, it is simply to help the person discover the posture they need to take in order to submit and surrender to Jesus.

"Dear Jesus, I am desperate to be rescued. I have sinned and need your forgiveness. Please forgive me and come into my life. I am inviting you today to be my Lord and leader. I want to live every day close to you and I look forward to spending eternity with you in heaven. Thank you. Amen."

Then you can welcome this young person into God's family, an adopted child of God who has been rescued from eternal darkness, starting this moment on Earth. Jesus promises a full life (John 10:10) and inseparable love (Romans 8:38–39) for those who believe, and that now includes another new believer.

Eternal Plan

Revisiting the conversation from the beginning of this chapter, after the online volunteer described the great divide to Kayla, she took a step of faith and asked, "What do you think? Is today the day you need to step onto that bridge, to cross that divide because of what Jesus did for you?"

The response read, "Absolutely. Of course, I want to do that."

That is the most common response we receive once they understand who Jesus is and what He offers. *Of course,* she said. You don't have to twist their arm.

As the redemption plan was laid out, Kayla embraced it and ended up praying to receive Christ. She invited Him to forgive her sin and she surrendered her life to Jesus.

And at the end of the chat, Julie circled back.

"Kayla, you came online and asked, 'Do I Matter?' Well, now that you know what God sees when He looks at you, let me ask you. 'Do you matter?'"

Kayla had come online asking a question, but her response to this inquiry was bold and confident. Her reply came in all caps with three exclamation points.

"I DO MATTER!!!"

A young woman, hurting and lost, doubtful anyone cared about her, discovered what Jesus sees when He looks at her. Beautiful. Loved. Valued. Prized. Specially created. And now she is bound for heaven.

Kayla is just one of the thousands who comes to the chatline at JesusCares.com looking for hope and purpose. Each one is desperate to know they are seen and heard and that they do matter. They think what they need is the approval of parents, peers, or partners, but what they really need to know is that God sees them as they are and loves them beyond measure, and that He has great plans for them. Eternal plans that He put into motion before the foundations of the world. Love and approval from our tribe is important, but the love of our heavenly Father is transformational. His embracing love changes question marks into exclamations and gives us a foundation to build on.

> What they really need to know is that God sees them as they are and loves them beyond measure, and that He has great plans for them.

Kayla's question was direct and simple. "Do I Matter?"

As soon as I saw that question for the first time, I was engaged. I wondered how many people I see daily, especially the twenty- and thirty-somethings, would ask the same question:

Do I Matter?

How many of them are crying out, some silently, for help?

Are you listening?

Can you see my pain?

I'm desperate; can you see me?

Building on the effectiveness of this online chat between Julie and

Kayla, we developed another website called www.DoIMatter.chat. Through our marketing, we reach out with the message: "If you feel invisible, unloved, or ignored, come explore what Jesus sees when He looks at you." Kids are logging in and lives are being rescued for eternity as they learn how beautifully and lovingly God views them.

Bottom Line in Action

I'd like to share another online dialogue to show you how the Rescue Plan can look in a conversation.

A young man named Carlos logged in to one of our websites, saying, "I need someone to pray for me."

Dan, one of our online volunteers, greeted Carlos by name and asked, "How are you today?"

"Not too good."

"Please tell me more. How can I pray for you?"

"I'm losing my family because of my bad choices in life."

Dan showed he was listening by offering an empathetic response. "I am really sorry to hear of your situation." He then told Carlos he would gladly pray for him, but first he asked, "Before I pray, Carlos, may I ask you a spiritual question?"

Carlos acknowledged he was open, so Dan gently pressed, "I know your heart is heavy over your marriage and your mistake. I am wondering about your relationship with Jesus. Who is Jesus to you?"

"My father," came Carlos's reply.

"Thank you for sharing that with me. I was 26 when I accepted Jesus as my Lord and Savior. He changed my life. Please tell me your story, Carlos."

"I need help. I'm 27 and I want to change my life around."

"I am here to help. I have started our chat talking about Jesus because I know He is where your help is going to come from. God loves you so much, Carlos."

The young man replied, "I need God in my life. I want to do better."

"I can help you find connection with Him. Rather than doing better, which is important, your first step in connecting with God and having a changed life is to humble yourself and realize you cannot fix you. Only God can do that. Do you want me to go on?"

"Yes."

"The first thing to grasp is who Jesus is and the reason He came to Earth. Jesus was God's rescue plan for humanity. So let's talk about why we need to be rescued. Everyone on the planet has sinned. I think you would agree."

"Yes."

"Here's the big problem with that. The Bible tells us the penalty for sin is death. Death is both our physical death as well as our spiritual death. Carlos, do you know what spiritual death is?"

"No."

"Death is eternal (as in forever) separation from God in hell. Many people think they can offset their sinful actions by being really good, trying harder, being religious, etc. That is false. We cannot undo our sin and make ourselves right with God. So… that is WHY Jesus came to Earth."

"Ok."

"He came to pay the 'death penalty' for our sin as a substitute so we could be forgiven by God.

"Here is God's plan laid out in John 3:16–18:

"God loved the people of this world so much that he gave his only Son, so that everyone who has faith in him will have eternal life and never really die. God did not send his Son into the world to condemn its people. He sent him to save them! No one who has faith in God's Son will be condemned. But everyone who doesn't have faith in him has already been condemned for not having faith in God's only Son."

"Oooo," came Carlos's reply as he began to understand the gospel message.

"So, the next question you might have is if we can't earn this salvation by trying harder, how do we get it?"

"Ask God to forgive us for our sins?"

"Yes, but the first step is receiving Jesus as your Lord and Savior. God offers this rescue plan as a free gift. Look at Ephesians 2:8–9—God saved you by His grace when you believed. And you can't take credit for this; it is a gift from God. Salvation is not a reward for the good things we have done, so none of us can boast about it.

"Here is the bottom line, Carlos. I will share with you God's instructions for connecting with Him and getting your sin forgiven. A fresh start in life. His instructions are found in Romans 10:9–10—*If you openly declare that Jesus is Lord and believe in your heart that God raised him from the dead, you will be saved. For it is by believing in your heart that you are made right with God, and it is by openly declaring your faith that you are saved.*" (NLT)

Carlos replied with a simple, "Ok."

Taking his cue from Carlos's continued positive responses, Dan continued. "So, now is decision time. Would you like me to lead you in a prayer of commitment, accepting Jesus Christ as your Lord and Savior?"

To which Carlos said, "Yes."

Dan wanted to make sure Carlos fully understood what he was saying yes to. "Before we pray, I have one question to ask you. After reading the Bible verses I have shared with you about why Jesus came to Earth, please tell me what you believe in your heart about Jesus."

"That He can save me."

"Okay. I will type a prayer and you can say my words back to God, or just use your own words. The big idea is to tell God what you believe about Jesus in your heart. Are you ready?"

Carlos replied yes, and Dan led the young man in an online prayer:

> "Father, I have read all the Bible verses Dan has shared with me tonight. I believe Jesus died on the cross in order to pay the death penalty for my sin and then rose from the dead on the third day.

I know I have sinned. I am really sorry, Father. Please forgive me and wash me clean.

Give me a new start.

Lord, if there is any way to keep me from losing my family, I ask you to intervene.

Thank you for saving me, Lord, and forgiving me. Please help me to live the remainder of my days in a way that honors you.

I love you, Lord. In Jesus' precious and holy name, I pray. Amen."

Carlos answered with "Amen."

"Did you pray?" asked Dan.

"Yes."

"Congratulations! On the authority of God's word, you are now a child of God. Look at John 1:12—*But to all who believed him and accepted him, he gave the right to become children of God.* (NLT) Welcome to the family of God, Carlos. You are now my brother in Christ!"

"Thanks, God!"

"Yes indeed! You have a new start. Look at 2 Corinthians 5:17—*This means that anyone who belongs to Christ has become a new person. The old life is gone; a new life has begun!*" (NLT) Dan went on to encourage Carlos to take some action toward developing in his new faith. "As a child of God," Dan taught, "there needs to be some new things in your life that reflect that." He asked

Carlos if he would like a recommendation for a church community and if he'd like a pastor to contact him, to which Carlos said yes. Then Dan told Carlos about the importance of starting to study the Bible and signed him up for free Bible studies via email.

With the promise to touch base the next day, Dan offered a few more words of encouragement before they signed off. "Carlos, God will begin to show you changes for your life. It won't happen all at once. As God shows you things to add to your life and remove, just obey. God loves you so much, Carlos, and I know He has great and mighty plans for your life. This is the first day of a brand-new life. You can never lose this awesome salvation. One day you and I will meet face-to-face in heaven. It will be awesome!"

"Amen. Thank you, Dan!"

"You are welcome, Carlos. God will see you through this difficult time. Have a blessed evening. I will write tomorrow. Bye for now."

And that's how one dedicated Jesus follower contended for a troubled Gen Z young man by following God's Rescue Plan.

Jesus paid the price so each one of us could be rescued from the Enemy and eternal separation from our loving, heavenly Father. God's Rescue Plan is for each of us—you, me, and every Millennial and Gen Z we meet. Every person needs to know that God loves them so much that He made a way so they could be rescued from hell and given entrance into heaven.

CHAPTER 11

Fully Captured

They will be called oaks of righteousness, a planting of the Lord for the display of his splendor (Isaiah 61:3b).

ONCE A young person makes the decision to accept Jesus into their life, where do they go from there? Once their attention has been fully captured and their focus has shifted toward a personal relationship with Jesus, what's next? How do we see their new commitment secured for eternity?

By now, this might not surprise you, but the number one goal is not church attendance. We don't comb the streets to recruit young people to fill our churches. The goal is to lead them to an intimate relationship with Jesus.

We want each new believer to realize they're loved by the Creator of the universe, to know they're never alone, to learn how to hear His whispers as they walk in their new faith with Him. Once they've said yes to a God who is bigger than their problems, they learn that even though all their questions might not be answered, God is in control of the outcomes. They can now believe He's always there to help, no matter how difficult their life gets. The goal is for them to live in the ongoing narrative of this beautiful relationship.

> Number one goal is not church attendance. The goal is an intimate relationship with Jesus.

So where does the church come in? I see the church community as the symptom of a healthy relationship with Christ. A young person will be more inclined to welcome a church community into their lives as their personal faith grows. Seems a bit like the old chicken and egg, doesn't it? How can they grow in their faith if they're not in the church? And what will it take to get them into the church so they can grow? Obviously, these young people need assistance to help them mature in their new faith. Spiritual growth rarely happens on its own.

I have two desires for every new believer. Number one is for them to know the importance of reading the Bible every day. Within 24 hours of giving their life to Christ, we want them starting a fresh pattern of daily Bible reading. They've expressed a desire to be close to God, and the Bible is the best way to learn about Him and grow closer to Him. The Bible is their lifeline; it's their source of knowledge and truth to direct their lives and to cling to in times of question and doubt.

The second desire is for them to be convinced of the need to connect with a local community of Christ followers. Preferably, this begins to happen within a week after turning their life over to Jesus. Imagine the safety they will experience when they connect with a faith-based group that looks like them, that loves Jesus like they do, a group they can begin to hang around with. That's where they start to grow.

Sunday morning is not always the best front door to the church. If we can get a new believer to connect with a faith-based peer group in the church, there is more of a magnetic draw. There will be more accountability and a better chance that they will continue to attend—and attending that peer group will move them toward the weekend services.

Groundwire offers new believers "growth tracks" where they can choose to have someone walk with them for the first several weeks of their spiritual journey. The growth tracks also offer more opportunity for them to engage in the online community to go deeper.

Our follow up goal at Groundwire is to see 30% of these new believers take a meaningful and measured step in their faith. In our ministry, we don't use the word discipleship, because we don't have enough interaction with these new believers to take them deep over long periods of time. Our calling is to reach lost youth where they are and lead them to Jesus; our mission doesn't include discipling these new believers and walking with them in their faith; however, we do want to give them the tools to help them grow, and try to get them to people who can take them deep as quickly as we can.

Somebody needs to.

That's why the need for others to join our mission is so critical. These young people who have made the decision to follow Christ require guidance, support, love. As new believers, they need active experience in the body of Christ, to be surrounded by mature Christians to remind them *God's got this and He'll never let go.*

No one organization or person can rescue and train the following generations on their own. That's why we're calling on you and the army of ordinaries God is preparing. The older generations can play a vital role in helping new believers grow into dynamic Christ followers.

Someone to Walk Alongside

If Bible reading is our first assignment, and connecting to a faith community is the second assignment, then connecting with a mentor would be assignment number three.

The third assignment, however, has proven to be more of a challenge and is part of the calling for writing this book. Millennials and Gen Z who have newly surrendered their hearts to Jesus would benefit greatly from a loyal relationship with a mentor. Up until recently, older mentors who are willing to invest in the next generation in these types of relationships have been hard to find. There haven't been a lot of mature Christians who are saying to the younger generations, *"Yes, I'll come alongside you and walk with you in your newfound faith."* A tremendous need is going unmet.

Part of the reason for that is because we have become dulled to the urgency. We live day-to-day in our established routines, while Millennials and Gen Z all around us are held captive by the Enemy outside our doors, destined for a life separated from God if something isn't done to rescue them.

We've also been tricked into believing kids are seeking entertainment, that they aren't willing to prioritize spiritual growth; that they seek fun, but will avoid depth. The kids themselves will tell us that's not true. A 23-year-old Gen Z told us recently that she sees an openness to Jesus in her generation, but *"not many are willing to guide those that are seeking."* Do you see the disconnect? We think they're not interested and they think we don't care.

But God is stirring the hearts of Baby Boomers and Gen X all over, and mentoring is becoming more of a widespread focus.

One mom was regularly texting Scriptures and words of encouragement to her teen daughter, when one day she accidentally responded to a group text with her daughter and one of her daughter's friends. Her message simply said, "I'm praying for you today!"

To this mom's surprise, the other young lady responded. "Thank you so much. I needed that encouragement today."

The accidental text and positive response made the mom wonder how many other kids would like to receive encouraging texts. So she added a couple more of her daughter's friends to the group, and every couple of days she would text them a Scripture, a word of hope, or a prayer, to let them know how important they are to God.

These young people responded eagerly to her messages, hungry for an adult to pay attention to them, to encourage them, even from a spiritual perspective. Because she wasn't being preachy, they were open. She reminded these young people how much God loved them and that He was always there for them.

Rather quickly, the group started to grow. The recipients of these loving texts kept telling others about them who then also wanted to be added to the list. Eventually, the mom's text chain grew to thirty or forty kids. It got to the point where she sent messages five days a week right after she dropped her kids off at school. If she ever went a couple of days without posting, the kids would reach out to her, wondering why they didn't hear from her. They missed receiving their Scripture or prayer or encouragement for even one day. Her intentional communications also opened the door for her to have meaningful conversations with many about their struggles, questions, and even their faith.

So is this mom mentoring? Yes, that's exactly what she's doing. She's investing in the lives of young people, being available, and reaching out to them on a regular basis. That's where mentoring begins.

Released in 2024, the movie *The Forge* tells the story of a local business leader who sees a lost, angry, young man with no purpose, and seeks him out, going so far as to offer a job in exchange for regular mentoring sessions. The business owner shows kindness, asks questions, listens, and eventually the troubled young man surrenders his life to Jesus. The movie goes on to reveal a long string of mentors and mentees, men young and old, who are growing in their faith together.

The scene of these men gathering in prayer and support represents a recognized need in our Christian community. Mentoring ministries and resources are beginning to spread across the Christian market. One example is MORE Mentoring, headquartered in Colorado, with materials to help train mentors on how to help young believers mature. This ministry is fervently praying and claiming the promise of one million mentors. They recognize the need for mentors is great.

It is time for us to ask ourselves the tough questions. What is our purpose in this season of life? What is our role in the kingdom of God as Boomers and Gen X? I want to tread this line carefully. It is not my intent to guilt anyone into action, but rather to expose the Enemy's strategies and inspire us to do something about it. He is stealing our kids and then making us feel unqualified to win them back. Every parent of a prodigal understands the feelings of hopelessness that accompany their child's spiritual demise. After years of trying to influence our kids, we can grow weary and tempted to throw in the towel. And that's right where the Enemy wants us. Discouraged and defeated.

The Enemy also wants us to lose eternal perspective and to ignore our purpose in this season of life. This happens so subtly in our modern-day; we become so consumed with meeting our own needs, especially in building careers and material wealth that we grow complacent in spiritual matters. And the closer we get to retirement, the greater the temptation to finally fill our days with whatever we want. After all, we've earned it, right? Again, the Enemy works hard to distract us with personal desires that have very little to do with God's plan for our lives.

Jesus spoke to this strategy directly when he said, *"Do not store up for yourselves treasures on Earth, where moths and vermin destroy, and where thieves break in and steal. But store up for yourselves treasures in heaven, where moths and vermin do not destroy, and where thieves do not break in and steal. For where your treasure is, there your heart will be also"* (Matthew 6:19–21). Let me ask you: What greater treasure is there than the rescued souls of a lost generation?

Although mentoring is not at the center of Groundwire's ministry, we believe strongly in its importance. I hope every mature Christian reader of this book will recognize the urgency of mentoring and seek God for opportunities to mentor these new young believers.

Model How It's Done

Another way to help young people grow in their faith is to model a life with Jesus for them. We can follow the apostle Paul's lead as he instructed the churches in Corinth, *"Follow my example, as I follow the example of Christ"* (1 Corinthians 11:1). We're telling young people by the way we live, "Follow me as I follow Christ." We don't point to Christ and say, "Now, go follow Him." Instead, we communicate to them, "I'm going to do my best to model what it looks like to follow Him. I'm so in love with Jesus that if you watch me, you'll see what that looks like.

I'm not perfect, but following Jesus truly is my priority." Young people who value authenticity as much as Millennials and Gen Z do need to see our authentic faith in action. We model what we believe every day, whether we are even aware of it or not.

> We're telling young people by the way we live, "Follow me as I follow Christ."

In 2020, when the pandemic hit, my wife, Jené, was a nurse leader at her hospital, and she was the one tasked with creating a COVID unit. Within 12 hours, she built the COVID unit at her hospital and had patients transferred into it. It was a whirlwind, chaotic, stressful time. In the beginning of the pandemic, hospitals weren't equipped with the right PPE gear, so Jené had to send her nurses into unsafe conditions. For months, she felt so uncomfortable sending nurses who she was responsible for into situations that weren't healthy for them, even potentially dangerous and life-threatening. As we can all recall, life for our healthcare workers was really difficult during that season.

In the midst of it all, Jené continued her personal pursuit of God. Every morning she prayed and surrendered to God, trusting in Him to help her through the difficult day ahead. She prayed, "God, I need your help. I need your support in this. I need your strength and courage." And then she headed to the hospital for another day of COVID unknowns.

As the pandemic wore on, multiple younger nurses noticed

Jené's example. She wasn't even aware they were watching until one of them told her, "I'm watching the grace you have as you live this out, the joy you have in this miserable situation."

Eventually, several people, hospital staff and patients, noticed Jené and the grace she displayed in such crazy times. They'd ask, "How are you staying resilient? How are you keeping your joy?" Jené took these opportunities to say, "Without God, I couldn't do it. But I keep my eyes focused on Him. I read Scripture every morning. I talk to Him every day. I ask Him for His best outcomes. And then I come in and work as if it was for Him and as if I was taking care of my family." Every day at the hospital, Jené modeled a life of walking with Jesus, and it was noticed.

The pandemic of 2020 lasted longer than anyone could have anticipated, creating chaos and uncertainty for the entire world. Many people rose as heroes during that time, especially in the healthcare industry. My wife's heroism extended beyond physical care. By being genuine in her faith, she also became a spiritual hero, someone the younger nurses admired.

Too many Millennials and Gen Z don't have spiritual heroes. Young people lack mature, healthy, inspiring Christians they can look up to, role models that make them say, *"I want the peace that guy has or that woman has. I want that same kind of joy in the midst of turmoil."* Their motivation for spiritual growth will increase if they can identify a spiritual hero and see something in their spiritual hero that they want for themselves.

Let them catch you.

We need to let the young people in our life catch us loving Jesus. It's not telling them to love Jesus. They need to catch us. They can't argue with our experience.

Sometimes leaders encourage young people to read the Bible, and then the young people never see the leader reading theirs. What a missed opportunity to model loving Jesus. How different would it be for young followers to walk in on their leader, at home, church, or at work, and catch them, proving they sincerely want to connect with God? I value the many times when my kids were younger and they would come downstairs to find me sitting in my chair, reading the Bible. They'd crawl into my chair with me, and we would read God's Word together. It wasn't a formal thing. They would just catch me.

I got caught another time that wasn't much fun, although it had its upside. As youth pastor, I was traveling with a team of teenagers from my youth group, and I got pulled over. We were on a long stretch of freeway near Mount Shasta in California. I mean, it was straightaway. There were no corners. There was no traffic. And I got pulled over because I was going 65 in a stretch with a posted 65 mph speed limit. However, the law in California was that if you're pulling any kind of a trailer, you can't go more than 55. Well, I had fifteen kids in the van and we were pulling a trailer.

I was a little frustrated because I hated that law. In my mind, I shouldn't have to go 55 when there's no reason to go 55. But I just sat there and kind of bit my tongue. I owned it and said, "Yes, officer, I was speeding. I knew I shouldn't have been." I joked with the highway patrolman while he wrote me a ticket.

As we pulled back onto the freeway, one of the young men in the van said, "You know, I always wanted to know what you would do if you got pulled over."

He'd been watching me. He wanted to know how I would deal with authority. Would I have a bad attitude or would I model a life surrendered to Jesus? I'm grateful God helped me bite my tongue back there on the side of the road. What I learned is they're always watching us, which is all the more reason for us to be sincere and devoted in our personal relationship with Jesus.

Let them challenge you.

One of my friends has served as CEO of some major companies. He is one of the most successful, impressive people in my world. So when he got let go unexpectedly from a company he'd been leading profitably, I flew out to spend some time with him. I assumed he'd be down and discouraged, and I wanted to encourage him. Instead, he inspired me.

He told me that getting fired was a blessing, not even a blessing in disguise but an obvious blessing after the shock wore off. He realized God had removed him from a toxic environment. By placing his trust in God, he wasn't destroyed but actually encouraged.

My friend's example of trusting God also paved the way of modeling his faith to the younger generation. When he called his daughter, who was in her mid-twenties at the time, to inform her he got fired, she didn't believe him at first. She finally realized he was indeed fired, and her comment revealed she'd been watching her father.

"Well, I guess now we'll see."

"See what?" he asked.

"Dad, you've been telling us our whole lives that our identity should not be locked up in our job, but it should be in Christ. Now we'll see if you're going to live what you've been teaching us."

My friend confessed to me the significance behind her challenge.

"For the past twenty-five years, practically my entire adult life, I've loved telling people what I do because my job is impressive. Now, for the first time, I don't have a business card. I'm just me."

This successful businessman and dad recognized the challenge and took it upon himself to pursue Jesus even more fervently. He wanted his identity planted squarely in God's plan for his life so his daughter could catch him modeling authentic faith in Jesus.

Spiritual Heroes

Like my friend, if we have a desire for our young people to love God, to be passionate about Him, then we want them to see that we're loving God, that we're pursuing Him, that we're chasing after Christ. The more we grow, the more the young people we're investing in will grow. They need spiritual heroes to look up to and learn from. But if they don't see us pursuing growth in our own faith, there's only one of two ways the young people in our life are ever going to grow beyond us. Either we start growing and give them opportunity to learn from our example, or they will choose another hero.

As Jesus washed the disciples' feet, he was setting an example for them. He clearly communicated the message that *"no servant is greater than his master"* (John 13:16). In the same way, a student can't learn more from their teacher than what the teacher knows. According to what Jesus is saying, we will be the ceiling to the young people who are following us.

Look at it from a skill perspective: If you're teaching a student math, they'll never get any better at math than you are. So, to be able to teach them more than you know, you have to educate yourself more. Or, secondarily, they will get better at math than you are if they choose another hero in that area, another teacher who can take them further. It's the same principle spiritually. If they're in your circle, they're watching you. And their prayer life will never be better than yours. Their passion for Christ will never be better than yours. Unless they choose another hero to follow, which sometimes happens. That's sad for us if they choose a more committed Christian to follow, but it's devastating when the other hero our kids choose is an ungodly figure who leads them in the wrong direction.

The main point here is to be continually growing in our own faith so we can lead these young believers forward in their new faith. The point isn't to build ourselves up in their eyes. That is the opposite of the message Jesus conveyed while he was on His knees washing the disciples' dirty feet. Following Jesus' example, He who is our greatest spiritual hero, we provide a solid model of loving Jesus, a model for the next generations to follow.

CHAPTER 12

The Power that Transforms

I urge, then, first of all, that petitions, prayers, intercession and thanksgiving be made for all people (1 Timothy 2:1).

NO ACTION we take toward contending for the younger generations is more important than prayer. We begin by interceding for all those who are lost and in captivity of the Enemy. We pray for ourselves to be the rescuers they need, asking for compassion, boldness, wisdom, strength, opportunities to share. And we pray for more harvesters, mature Christians around the world to be called to go, to reach our kids, all kids, for Jesus.

We can't do any good for anybody without the work of the Holy Spirit, and we're not meant to. Young people today are trapped in the belief they have to do it all on their own. We know how false that is. We know we can't do it all on our own and that God is always with us to accomplish His perfect will. God calls us to participate in His great Rescue Plan through His guidance and power. That's why we pray.

Pray for the Younger Generations

Prayer is more than a powerful thing to do. Prayer is an act of obedience to God. Samuel understood well the importance of being obedient to pray. After Saul was appointed king, the Israelites saw the error of their ways and pleaded with Samuel to pray for them. His answer? *"Far be it from me that I should sin against the Lord by failing to pray for you"* (1 Samuel 12:23). What this says to us is that if we're not praying for those God has entrusted to us, we're sinning against God. We picture sin as overt sin, but we need to understand that if we don't take our place as the spiritual protectors for those God has entrusted to us, if we fail to pray for them and the people in our sphere of influence, we're sinning against God. And the next generations are left exposed to evil's influence as a result.

Our world has been infiltrated by the Enemy, and our kids are being sucked into His deceitful lies. Modern culture pulls at young people, trying to convince them Christianity is false, that the Bible is a myth, and that they can determine the course of their own lives. They are indeed trapped in the battle, and prayer is our number one weapon for getting them out. We need to pray persistently they see the Truth, the Life, and the Way—their path to freedom.

Let's look at what happens when we pray. God answers prayers that are in line with His will, and we know His will includes the salvation of every person. He doesn't want *"anyone to perish, but everyone to come to repentance"* (2 Peter 3:9).

I recently had a conversation with a mom who discovered her defiant seventeen-year-old daughter Addison was involved in a dating relationship she'd not known about. The teen was also going to parties behind her mom's back and started smoking. This wise mom told me that the first thing she did when she found out about Addison's secret was pray.

> No action we take toward contending for the younger generations is more important than prayer.

It began not as a prayer of great faith, but as one of "Oh God, what's going on? Please help!" But as this mom and her husband sought God's guidance, their desperate cry for help turned into a prayer of confidence:

"God, we know you are in control of the situation. Right now, we are standing against all the powers of the Enemy that are attacking our daughter and our family. We stand in God's anointing and we take the authority that has been given to us by God to lead this family. We refuse to let rebellion and lies drag our daughter away. God, give us wisdom. Help us to communicate with our daughter. Take the blinders off her eyes. Protect her, draw her close to you, and bring our little girl back into submission—first to you and then to us."

With confidence, they entered Addison's room right before bedtime. They told her they knew about her behavior. When Addison tried to argue with them, they refused to hear it. The conversation went on for quite some time and ended with hugs and tears. Addison admitted she had been hiding things from her parents and asked for forgiveness.

Their relationship became even more open, and now Addison is doing well and getting more involved in spiritual pursuits.

Although I love the end of the story, I also love the middle. This mom knew it wasn't great parenting that made Addison hear them out and realize her attitude and actions were wrong. She knew it was the spiritual authority they had received from God as they asked for His wisdom and direction that overcame Addison's combative spirit. Point blank, God answered their prayer. He intervened in the way He does, to soften a hardened heart and loose the shackles that bind. Again, this is why we pray.

We must pray aggressively and often.

Imagine the power of prayer for all the Millennials and Gen Z who are oppressed and bound by spiritual strongholds. We must pray aggressively and often. Let us ask God to intervene on behalf of our young people, for we know that without His help nothing positive will be accomplished. In prayer, we can give the young person we're praying for to the Lord and rest in the fact that God is able to keep that which we trust to Him. Remember to always fight for the young person in the spiritual arena before you engage in conversation. Never try to engage with them without praying first.

Pray for their salvation and pray for their continued spiritual growth, so the Enemy won't be able to take them back once they've been rescued.

My favorite prayer to pray for young people is Ephesians 3:16–19: *"I pray that out of his glorious riches he may strengthen you with power through his Spirit in your inner being, so that Christ may dwell in your hearts through faith. And I pray that you, being rooted and established in love, may have power, together with all the Lord's holy people, to grasp how wide and long and high and deep is the love of Christ, and to know this love that surpasses knowledge—that you may be filled to the measure of all the fullness of God."*

I especially love the part about God helping them be rooted and established in His love, because if a young person is rooted and established in His love, they're impossible to manipulate. If they're just aware of His love and aren't walking fully in it, they're vulnerable to manipulation. For example, if somebody comes alongside a young person who isn't rooted and established in God's love and seduces them with an untruth—like a young man trying to woo a girl by saying "I love you,"—they're easy to manipulate. But if they are rooted and established in God's love as their premier way of life, they'll see right through the lies and not compromise their convictions.

The Bible teaches that it is through God's will and His work in people's lives that they learn to reject the wrong things, embrace the right ones, and be positive influences on others. *"For the grace of God has appeared that offers salvation to all people. It teaches us to say 'No' to ungodliness and worldly passions, and to live self-controlled, upright and godly lives in this present age"* (Titus 2:11–12). We can pray with authority and confidence, knowing we are praying in agreement with God's will for each young person on our prayer list.

One effective prayer strategy is inserting into a Bible verse the name of the young person you're praying for. For example, you can use as a guide the adaptation of Paul's prayer in Ephesians 1:17–19. *"Lord, I thank you for [name of individual you're praying for]. God, I ask you to give her the spirit of wisdom and revelation so that she may know you better. I pray also that the eyes of her heart will be enlightened so that she may know the hope to which she's been called, to the riches that are hers, and the incomparably great power that is available to her."* Personalizing prayers like this encourages our faith as we persist in intercession.

We can also let young people know we're praying for them. If they don't know Jesus yet, they will probably just be grateful to know you care enough to pray. And if they are walking with Jesus, wherever they are on their faith journey, they will value your prayerful investment in their lives.

One of my friends bought a study Bible that he intended to give to his Millennial daughter. Over the next 12 months, he used that Bible as he did his devotions, going from Genesis through Revelation. As he read, he highlighted verses and wrote notes to her like, "This scripture made me think of you because of your kind heart toward children," and "I love this passage where it talks about people listening to Jesus with delight." He wanted his daughter to see Jesus the way he did. One year later, he wrapped the Bible and gave it to her as a gift. As she opened it, he told her, "I prayed for you every day over this past year as I read this." The daughter treasured the Bible and benefited from the prayers her father prayed on her behalf.

Prayer is our number one weapon for defeating the Enemy in contending for the next generations. Let us be praying for the brokenhearted, the ones Gilda and Jorge saw at Six Flags, the kids at basketball games, every youth walking down the street who is lost and overwhelmed.

Pray for Harvesters—Jesus' Own Words

Earlier we looked closely at Jesus' directive in Matthew 9:38, a directive that applies to all Jesus followers today. With intense compassion for the harassed and helpless people who were lost like sheep without a shepherd, He told His guys to "ask the Lord of the harvest, therefore, to send out workers into his harvest field". Basically, He was telling them to pray for more people to go and share the gospel message. These were Jesus' own words to "ask the Lord" to send out more workers.

I'm amplifying Jesus' prayer request because it is the key to kingdom harvest. May your prayers lead to mature Christians around the world being filled with God's heart for a lost generation of kids and rising up with His courage and wisdom. Ask God to provide opportunities to share His truth with those who are hurting and confused. Pray for His divine intervention to place people together at just the right place and time so those beginning conversations can start happening. And then trust Jesus to lead the harvesters He is calling, just as He is calling mentors, spiritual heroes and role models, and intercessors.

One of the interesting things in this command is that He instructs His followers to pray, but He also invites us to answer that prayer. We will discover more opportunities to share Jesus when we are praying that people would be aggressively sharing. We will develop more compassion as we ask God to move people toward the harvest fields because of growing compassion.

We all know that we should "go" and God sometimes uses our prayers to give us more passion, more motivation, and more awareness. We sometimes become the answer to the very prayers we are praying.

> We sometimes become the answer to the very prayers we are praying.

Pray With Me

I spoke at a gathering not long ago, and the Holy Spirit stirred this prayer within me as we prayed for our generation and the generations to follow. I'd like to invite you to pray it with me again. I believe this prayer involves all of us.

Father, in the name of Jesus thank You for sending Jesus to this Earth. Lord, we thank You for taking that initiative that You didn't wait for us to get to You. You knew we couldn't, so you sent Him.

In that same manner, thank You, Jesus, for suffering for us. But God, we don't just want to be saved and safe. God, we are willing to step into the battle and we're willing to opt into conversations.

God, the majority of people in our nation who are unchurched are waiting for somebody to introduce them to the God who can make sense out of their chaos. You are that God and we are willing to be an instrument that You use.

So God, stir us. Allow us to take meaningful steps. Break our hearts. Give us eyes to see their need, what they're struggling with, what they're going through. Give us compassion so that we can't ignore them.

And God, give us the skills that we need to have meaningful conversation with them about Your Son. And I pray, God, for people who long to be used in this way. God, I pray that You give them those opportunities and they would begin to celebrate the opportunity that you've given them to share Jesus in meaningful ways.

God, we believe You are still good. God, we are convinced the gospel is still powerful. God, we are convinced the harvest is still ripe. God, move in our nation. Rescue a generation. In Jesus' name we pray, Amen.

My fellow Christ followers, I ask you to join me in repeating this prayer on behalf of the younger generations. They need Jesus desperately. And only through praying diligently will we be able to help them find Him.

CHAPTER 13

Time to Take Action

So is my word that goes out from my mouth: It will not return to me empty, but will accomplish what I desire and achieve the purpose for which I sent it (Isaiah 55:11).

I'M A basketball enthusiast, and one of my bucket list items has always been to go see Duke play basketball. I fell in love with Duke when I was a kid and I've wanted to see them play in their home arena pretty much my whole life. Thanks to a friend of mine, I was gifted a couple of tickets to Cameron Indoor Stadium to be in the house and watch Duke vs. Florida State a couple of years ago. I invited another basketball friend, and we showed up an hour before the game was scheduled to start. The place was already packed. The whole building felt like it was vibrating with the energy in the room. They call the student section the Cameron Crazies—and it was CRAZY! Students were all having a great time. They knew every lyric to every song. Our seats were near the standing room only student section behind the backboard. Kids were jammed in, moving in unison to the pre-game music. As the players warmed up, I watched the students. They were squeezed in tight, with nose touching the hair of the person in front of them. The players were locked in and the students were cheering them on... when suddenly a thought hit me that shocked me to my core.

I remembered a statistic that I had been praying over for a year or so. It says that only one in five people in their generation could tell you how to become a Christian. Only one in five can tell you that it's because of a relationship with Jesus. So as I stood with the Duke crowd, I thought, *If that's true, then four out of five of these kids would go to hell.*

I started to count. Not individuals, but rows... one, two, three, four. In my mind, the first four rows sat down, leaving the fifth row standing. I elbowed the guy with me.

"Hey, listen to what I'm thinking about." I shared the one in five statistic with him, and then said, "Man, if that stat's true, then 80% of those kids don't know Jesus."

The energy in our Duke-hyped moment dropped in that instant.

He kind of frowned at me. "Yeah, thanks for doing that." It was such a heavy thought in that moment.

However, literally two to three minutes later, the ball went in the air, the game started, and I immediately forgot about the heaviness I was feeling.

After the game, my friend and I talked about it on our ride back to the airport. The Lord reminded me how easy it is for me to forget the spiritual reality, because I can so easily get locked up in my entertainment and my own interests. I get so distracted with those things, whereas I should be thinking about those people who are lost and who are bound for hell. I repeat often about young people: They're either going to celebrate through eternity or they're going to suffer through it. But so quickly at the ball game, I went from really being overwhelmed with all the kids in the arena bound for an eternity of suffering to forgetting it all together. God convicted me. He reminded me that life is too short to waste and eternity is too long to ignore. Since that Duke game, my prayer has been, "God, don't ever let me forget the true ramifications and the true spiritual realities of somebody's relationship with Jesus and what it means to them."

We have the opportunity to make as big of a difference in lives as we can. And if we take care of somebody emotionally, that's great. If we take care of their physical need, it's great. I'm telling you right now, though; the only thing that lasts is when somebody has transferred from death to life, from darkness into light. That's when they will get to spend eternity with Jesus. If we want God to use us, we are going to have to stop watching lost and hurting young people pass us by and we are going to have to start leading them to Jesus.

But that won't happen without a fight, and I'm here to tell you the Enemy is all in.

We Can't Be Passive

John 10:10 tells us the thief is on a focused mission. We as the church must wake up and realize we're on a mission too, because the

Enemy has come to steal, kill, and destroy. The Enemy is aggressive. The church cannot afford to be passive. Lives are on the line.

The enemy is aggressive. The church cannot afford to be passive

---

Not long ago, my wife and I stumbled across an article that had us shaking our heads in disbelief. It seems some content creators are developing videos with instructions and encouragement to commit suicide. After a tutorial on how to slit your wrists for maximum damage, one video ends with the personality turning toward the camera and saying, "Just end it!" In essence his message is "*When life hurts, choose death!*"

You are probably handling this with the same amount of shock and disgust as we were. Jené and I looked at each other and didn't even know what to say. How do you process that kind of darkness? But over the next few minutes, I remembered the urgency behind our mission. If darkness is that aggressive, shouldn't we be even more? If worldly culture is preying on hopelessness, anxiety, and mental health, telling people how to cause pain to those around, shouldn't we amplify Jesus, the One who offers hope, peace, love, and salvation? Don't you think we should work just as hard, be just as committed, and speak just as boldly?

The Enemy is working overtime to amplify pain, steal hope, and torture hurting souls. In the New York City Drag Queen parade in June 2023, transgender participants chanted "We're here, we're queer, and we're coming for your children," enraging Christian parents across the country. Parents were right to be angry, but the LGBTQ community, or queer agenda, is not our enemy. The real Enemy is the devil who taunts with his threats: *I'm here, I'm aggressive, and I'm coming for your kids.*

Seeing the source of evil clearly, no parent would sit back and say, "You know what? We're okay with our sons and daughters being lied to, killed, stolen, and destroyed." But our kids are sent into danger zones all the time. Our culture is rife with ungodly, anti-Christ influence. We must fight on that front.

After I read the article about the suicide tutorial and got past my initial disgust, my jaw tightened, my prayers became more focused, and my determination to be a voice of truth and hope grew.

They say, "When Life Hurts, choose death," but I will boldly proclaim, "When Life Hurts, consider Jesus." For He is the answer to every meaningful question you will ever ask, and He is the One who offers abundant and eternal life.

When I look back at those students at the Duke basketball game, I can picture passionate, mature Christians talking with them one at a time until they've all been reached. Every time one has been rescued I picture us going back for one more.

The movie *Hacksaw Ridge*[31] is the true story of Pfc. Desmond T. Doss, a soldier who went into WWII as a combat medic. Because

---

31. Hacksaw Ridge, directed by Mel Gibson (2016, Summit Entertainment, Lionsgate)

he was a pacifist, he wouldn't carry a gun. The other American soldiers made fun of him and mocked him because of his beliefs. But he stayed true to his convictions, despite the ridicule and the danger to his own safety. Then, in the bloodiest battle of the war, Doss's troop is engaged in active gunfire on Hacksaw Ridge in Okinawa. His team is getting cut down, so they retreat back down the massive cliff they had climbed up to attack the Japanese. The entire regiment retreats, but Doss stays to rescue fellow soldiers who had been injured. Over the course of five hours, with his hands bleeding, he lowers the wounded soldiers down, one at a time. And every time he prays, "Lord, help me get one more. Just one more!" It is estimated Doss, without a gun but with extraordinary determination, rescued seventy-five men during the horrific battle.

How many young people can our army of ordinaries rescue from an eternity of suffering if we go into the raging battle with the same fervor and conviction as this young private? Let us pray for God to fill our hearts with His compassion for every lost soul and the strength to persevere until they're all pulled from danger into His safety.

Appointed Time in History

"From one man he made all the nations, that they should inhabit the whole Earth; and he marked out their appointed times in history and the boundaries of their lands. God did this so that they would seek him and perhaps reach out for him and find him, though he is not far from any one of us" (Acts 17:26–27).

The Good News Translation uses the word *"exact,"* that God *"fixed beforehand the exact times"* and places (v. 26). Why did He do that? So that men everywhere would reach out and find Him; He's not far from any of us. As He was designing us in our mother's wombs, God knew our purpose and the specific circumstances in each of our lives as adults.

> God knew exactly the cultural, political, and technological season we'd be in, and He put you here—at this time and in this place for a purpose.

God knew exactly the cultural, political, and technological season that we'd be in, and He put you here—at this time and in this place for a purpose. He knew exactly when you'd be here and exactly where you'd be. He knew who you'd be around, that you'd have opportunities and a relationship with Him. He did all this because He wants you to point others toward Him. And He knows exactly what He can do through you if you are intentional with Him.

There are two types of personal evangelists that I have seen—those who are accidental and those who are intentional. Those who hope they have a conversation of significance and those who are looking to begin a conversation. A lot of people want to make a difference… if someone comes asking… but those who are intentional will be used by God in amazing ways.

So this is my prayer for you and me: "God, give me a strategy!" We can't wait until somebody walks up to us and just happens to fall to their knees and cry out, "I'm going to hell. Can you help me find Jesus?" Our purpose is to point others to Him. We must push past the fear of taking the first step. I encourage you to pray for opportunities and then look for them. Listen for the pain or hopelessness in the conversations you have. Keep your eyes open for those who are struggling, and when you find them, don't just pat the person on the back and tell them you will pray for them. Take the time and introduce them to the One who can meet every need. God knew what He was doing when He put us here and now. He has a purpose for each of us, and He's calling us to intentionality.

Roughly thirty years ago (man, I am getting old) I used to spend a lot of time at the local rec center. This served two purposes. First, I really do love to play basketball. Second, I wanted to be around young people in an environment where their walls were not up.

One of the young men that I befriended was a sophomore at the local high school. He also loved basketball. Over the course of several weeks, I started to work with him on the court. Showed him some tricks of the trade.

After investing hours with him, we sat down to rest, and I asked him about his family. "How long have you lived in my town? How many siblings do you have? What do your parents do for work?" When I found out that his parents were divorced, I empathized and told him I was sorry. I could relate. "That is hard. How are you doing with that?" When he told me he was coping, I knew that it was more difficult than he let on.

When the time was right, I asked him if he ever turned to God or talked to Him when he was alone. He told me he believed in God, but he didn't know how to talk with Him.

Now, we were cooking. He didn't put up walls. He didn't turn and run. He didn't try to change the subject. He wanted to know the God who could help him through the chaos of his life.

Because he was open, I said, "One of the things that blows me away is not that God will let me talk to Him, but that He will actually listen. And I have learned that He will actually talk to me. He whispers peace and hope to my heart and He helps carry me through my struggles."

My young friend was obviously intrigued, so I continued. "I am talking about a personal relationship with the God of Creation, not just church attendance."

"What does that look like?" he asked.

I started at the beginning. I shared God's Rescue Plan that starts with the problems of separation and penalty for sin and ended with the solution. Jesus' willing sacrifice on the cross for our sin led me to saying, "All it takes is a recognition that I am desperate for a Savior and an acknowledgment that God provided one." After a pause to ensure it had sunken in, I asked him, "So what do you think? Do you want to receive His gift and begin the most amazing relationship you will ever know?"

Without hesitation, he said, "Absolutely, I think this is what I have been looking for."

That day, sitting against the wall in the gym, he began a relationship with Jesus and it transformed his life.

I believe all of us will have amazing stories to tell. Stories of countless young people being rescued from an eternity of darkness—kids and grandkids, neighbors, employees, waitresses, complete and random strangers—because kingdom-minded Christ followers are waking up and taking action. We're no longer willing to sit back and passively let the Enemy kill, steal, and destroy our children. We are rallying and equipping an army under God's leadership.

No More Excuses

We can't let our excuses keep us on the sidelines when the Enemy has no shame, is recruiting ambassadors daily, and is blatantly trying to destroy entire generations. As devoted followers of Christ and mature human beings, we must work to overcome the excuses that keep us from being a part of God's rescue team.

We are moved by the things we are convinced of, and if you are absolutely convinced that heaven and hell are real, that God offers eternal life, and that people will either suffer through eternity or they will celebrate through it, then you will be moved to speak up. But if we are more afraid of rejection than we are concerned for those who are lost, if we find ourselves avoiding conversations about Jesus, this is where we need to stop embracing those excuses and pray, *"God, help me to be truly convinced that Jesus is the only way to God."* We can't afford to keep our mouth shut when God opens the door for us.

For those who still feel uneasy going through the process of engaging in conversation and leading another person to Christ, I encourage you to practice. Perhaps recruit a friend and take turns doing role playing of spiritual conversations. Don't let inexperience stand in the way of initiating these important dialogues.

Remember that it's a bold-faced lie that the younger generations don't want to hear about Jesus. Our adversary wants us to remain convinced they aren't open. Too many Christians have embraced this lie, and it keeps them from sharing Jesus with those who need Him most. The truth is, they do want to have meaningful conversations, they do want people to take an interest in their life, and they do want people to point them toward the One who is the answer. In my experience, most young people long for someone to stop long enough to say "I care," and they are very open when that caring person shares their source of hope.

We met the kind of caring person I'm describing back in Chapter 1: Anne, the online volunteer, who responded to a young woman on the verge of swallowing a pile of pills.

When Megan logged on that day, she had no idea an "Oh honey" grandma would respond to her plea for help. That's my nickname for Anne. She is a sweet old lady who says things like, "Oh honey, you have a great future" and "Oh honey, you're never alone. Jesus is always there for you."

Anne shared with the desperate young woman, "Megan, I know what it feels like to be broken, and I am here to tell you, Jesus is more than ready to heal your hurts and give you such peace and purpose… He is for you! He will never leave or forsake you!" So yes, Anne is what I like to call an "Oh honey" grandma, but to the Enemy, Anne is a dangerous threat. She has rescued many wounded young people, one at a time, much like private Doss at Hacksaw Ridge.

Not long after Anne and Megan's online conversation happened, I read their transcript on the plane on my way to Orange County, and I was so moved. I realized Anne lives in the Inland Empire, which was just minutes from where my Tuesday lunch had canceled. So I arranged to go meet Anne.

As I walked into her home, she did what grandmas do. She gave me a big hug. She fed me cookies and milk. And then she said, "Thank you. You don't know what Groundwire has meant to me. I'm a shut in. My mom has dementia and my husband has Parkinson's. I only get out of the house three hours a week. The only part of my day that I look forward to is when I put everybody to bed, and I log in and I get to tell people about my Jesus."

I asked if I could see where she did her online conversations. She took me to her office, where I saw a long wicker basket. It was filled with five-by-seven cards of every chat she'd had over the last eighteen months. I flipped through them and contact information, prayer requests, and notes from their chats. Then she handed me Megan's card since we had just talked about it.

Megan's was rubber banded to a thick stack.

"Why is this one rubber banded?" I asked her.

She looked at the ground and humbly, almost embarrassed, answered, "Those are the ones the Lord's allowed me to introduce to Him so far."

"How many?"

"Eighty-one."

That was ten years ago and as of this writing she's still coaching with us.

One life at a time.

The Day Is Coming

I was speaking at a university for an off-site event put on by some workers on the campus. They invited me to speak once a quarter and were drawing 700–800 college students every Tuesday night. The meetings were a Spirit-filled experience with great worship.

This night, God was moving before I got up to speak. I could sense the electric presence of the Lord in the worship. As we sang the song "He is Mighty to Save," I felt God kind of elbow me in the gut. He said, "Now is the time of salvation." Before I was supposed to be introduced, I walked to the front to the microphone. The worship team continued to play in the background while I spoke.

"Listen," I began. "Some of you, you sing this song. And you know that God is mighty to save, but you haven't surrendered to Him yet. Some of you have been watching what God is doing.

You've been excited about the concept that God wants to be an active part of your whole life. But yet you have not yet taken that step. You haven't crossed that line of faith and said, 'Okay, God, I'm yours.'" I was moving toward a call to salvation, but before I could say anything else, kids started to run to the front, all the way from the back of the auditorium. It was the time of salvation for them. They had been watching it. They had been experiencing it. They'd been holding back. They had excuses and all of a sudden in one quick moment, God broke through and it turned into a massive response as the Holy Spirit offered salvation.

The reason I share this story is to show you there's a younger generation that's been looking for something and they're seeing; they just haven't responded yet. But there's coming the day where they're going to run to the front. There just needs to be somebody there to tell them what they're running to.

Time For Us to GO

"I tell you, open your eyes and look at the fields! They are ripe for harvest" (John 4:35).

Millennials and Gen Z are desperate for Jesus and they're waiting for us to cross the street, to come to where they are. I never want to hear another young person say, "How is it possible that no one has ever told me God loves me?" I'm praying that God would stir within each of us an inability to ignore the spiritual needs of the young people around us, that we would see Millennials and Gen Z with clear eyes. I'm asking God to help us see their brokenness and loneliness and hurt, and that God would develop in us the skill set and the ability to speak into those situations. May God lead us as we draw them into meaningful conversations about the gospel in a way that their barrier goes down and their desire for Jesus goes up.

Following a recent speaking event, I was speaking with someone in the back when a gentleman walked up to us and asked to meet me.

The guy next to me said, "Oh, you don't know Sean? He's the guy who introduces people to Jesus and tells them how to get to heaven."

Wow, I'll own that. I'm okay with it, because that's my passion. And I pray that is your passion, too.

Jesus' last words on Earth before He ascended into heaven spoke a specific message to His disciples, and they still ring loud and clear for us today. *"He said to them, 'Go into all the world and preach the gospel to all creation'"* (Mark 16:15). Perhaps if Jesus were here with us right now at this appointed time in history, He might add, "Go! I have called you to contend for a generation. Satan wants to sway Millennials and Gen Z into his camp of misery, but you can capture them with my gospel message instead. I love them and I don't want to lose a single one. So… in my name, GO!"

It is time we head into the fields and share the foundational truth of God's love. We see them for who they are and we understand their pain and confusion. Our message is clear: The Enemy wants to steal, kill, and destroy them, but Jesus loves them and wants them to live an abundant life with and through Him. Let's go where they are and show them how to know Jesus and how to get to heaven. Together, our army of ordinaries can liberate entire generations for eternity. I pray we will be known as "The Generation Who Led Millions to Jesus."

These are exciting times! God is on the move. The harvest is ripe. LET'S GO.

God's Rescue Plan

The Problem

1. We have all sinned and missed God's standard, which is perfection.
2. The penalty for sin, according to the Bible, is spiritual death.
3. Spiritual death is eternal separation from God in a prison called hell.
4. We cannot fix our sin problem by trying to be good or by becoming religious.

The Solution

5. Jesus, who is God, had no sin of His own.
6. He came to Earth to pay the death penalty for our sin.
7. He died, was buried, and rose from the dead, victorious over sin and death.
8. God says whoever will repent, believe this message, be willing to surrender their all to Christ Jesus, will have all their sins forgiven, washed clean, and guaranteed heaven when they die.

Bible verses that reveal God's Rescue Plan

- For all have sinned and fall short of the glory of God, and all are justified freely by his grace through the redemption that came by Christ Jesus (Romans 3:23–24).
- For the wages of sin is death, but the gift of God is eternal life in Christ Jesus our Lord (Romans 6:23).
- But your iniquities have separated you from your God; your sins have hidden his face from you, so that he will not hear (Isaiah 59:2).
- God saved you by his grace when you believed. And you can't take credit for this; it is a gift from God. Salvation is not a reward for the good things we have done, so none of us can boast about it (Ephesians 2:8–9, NLT).
- God made him who had no sin to be sin for us, so that in him we might become the righteousness of God (2 Corinthians 5:21).
- Jesus gave his life for our sins, just as God our Father planned, in order to rescue us from this evil world in which we live (Galatians 1:4, NLT).
- Christ died for our sins according to the Scriptures, that he was buried, that he was raised on the third day according to the Scriptures (1 Corinthians 15:3–4).
- God loved the people of this world so much that he gave his only Son, so that everyone who has faith in him will have eternal life and never really die. God did not send his Son into the world to condemn its people. He sent him to save

them! No one who has faith in God's Son will be condemned. But everyone who doesn't have faith in him has already been condemned for not having faith in God's only Son (John 3:16–18 cev).

- If you openly declare that Jesus is Lord and believe in your heart that God raised him from the dead, you will be saved. For it is by believing in your heart that you are made right with God, and it is by openly declaring your faith that you are saved (Romans 10:9–10 NLT)

Millennial and Gen Z Statistics

- 83% of the younger generations said moral truth depends on the circumstances, and only 6% said moral truth is absolute.[32]
- Only 30% of young people (18–34) say pastors have high or very high standards of moral and ethics.[33]
- Gen Z gets 91% of their news from social media.[34]
- 46% of Gen Z feel stressed or anxious "most of" or "all of" the time.[35]
- Statistics show 90% of substance use disorders (SUDs) start during the teenage years.[36]

32. Barna Group. (n.d.). Americans Are Most Likely to Base Truth on Feelings. Barna. https://www.barna.com/research/americans-are-most-likely-to-base-truth-on-feelings/

33. Earls, A. (2024, January 24). Public Trust of Pastors Hits New Record Low. Lifeway Research. http://research.lifeway.com/2024/01/24/public-trust-of-pastors-hits-new-record-low/

34. University of Chicago. (2022, August 31). Fatigue, traditionalism, and engagement: news habits and attitudes of the Gen Z and Millennial generations. AP NORC. https://apnorc.org/projects/fatigue-traditionalism-and-engagement-news-habits-and-attitudes-of-the-gen-z-and-millennial-generations/

35. Mental health today. A deep dive based on the 2023 Gen Z and Millennial survey. Deloitte. (2023, May). https://www2.deloitte.com/content/dam/Deloitte/mt/Documents/about-deloitte/deloitte-2023-genz-millennial-survey-mental-health.pdf

36. Gomez, S. (2024, April 15). Gen Z and Addiction. Addiction Center. https://www.addictioncenter.com/addiction/gen-z-addiction/

- The number one place Gen Z goes to for help with depression and anxiety is not a therapist, a teacher, a pastor, or a parent. The number one place they go to find help or relief is TikTok.[37]
- 70% believe the American church is irrelevant.[38]
- Average Gen Z has 8.5 social media accounts in their name.[39]
- Only 4% of Gen Z have a biblical worldview compared to 10% of Millennials.[40]
- Nearly 1 in 3 Gen Z struggles with anxiety, depression, or other mental health challenges and suicide rates have drastically risen.[41]
- Only 34% of Gen Z believes that churches have a positive impact on society, compared to 55% of Baby Boomers.[42]

37. Garnham, C. (2022, September 1). The Gen Z Mental Health save-what is causing the surge?. HealthMatch. https://healthmatch.io/blog/the-gen-z-mental-health-wave-what-is-causing-the-surge

38. Rainer, T., & Rainer, J. (2009). The Millennials: Connecting to America's Largest Generation. B&H Publishing Group.

39. Kakadia, K. (2023, March 30). A comprehensive list of social media statistics for journalists. Sociallyin Insider. https://blog.sociallyin.com/social-media-statistics-for-journalists-by-sociallyin

40. Morrow, Jonathan. (2024). Only 4 Percent of Gen Z Have a Biblical Worldview. https://www.impact360institute.org/articles/4-percent-gen-z-biblical-worldview/

41. American Psychological Association, Stress in Americaä. (2020). https://www.apa.org/news/press/releases/stress/2020/report-october/

42. Cox, Daniel A. (2024) "Generation Z and the Future of Faith in America"; https://www.americansurveycenter.org/research/generation-z-future-of-faith/

- 1 in 5 Gen Z identifies as LGBTQ, the highest percentage of any generation, reflecting a major shift in how they perceive identity and sexuality.[43]
- 77% of Gen Z say they are open to the existence of God or a higher power or express curiosity about spiritual matters.[44]
- 74% of Gen Z says they want to grow spiritually, showing that despite cultural challenges, there's a hunger for deeper faith experiences.[45]
- According to recent studies, while nearly half of Gen Z individuals report having made a commitment to Jesus, only a small percentage (around 13%) are considered "biblically engaged".[46]
- 7 hours 22 minutes a day on the phone…ABC News[47]
- 7% of Millennials and 13% of Gen Z are atheists.[48]

43. Jones, Jeffery M. (2024) "LGBT Identification in U.S. Ticks up to 7.1%" https://news.gallup.com/poll/389792/lgbt-identification-ticks-up.aspx/

44. Kinnaman, David. (2024) "Rising Spiritual Openness in America" https://www.barna.com/research/rising-spiritual-openness/

45. Ibid.

46. Fulks, J., Petersen, R., & Plake, J. F. (2022). State of the Bible 2022. American Bible Society.

47. Jacobo, J. (2019, October 29). Teens spend more than 7 hours on screens for entertainment a day: Report. ABC News. https://abcnews.go.com/US/teens-spend-hours-screens-entertainment-day-report/story?id=66607555

48. Atheism doubles among generation Z. Barna Group. (2023, August 16). https://www.barna.com/research/atheism-doubles-among-generation-z/

- Statistics show 71% of Millennials and 64% of Gen Z believe in God.[49]
- By 2023, statistics from the quality-of-life questions reveal young people answered negatively between 48%–52% of the time.[50]
- Nearly one-third of Gen Z (32%) are regularly engaged in activism or social justice work (compared to 24% of millennials), demonstrating a significant Gen Z commitment to societal change. This engagement deepens among college students, where the percentage escalates to nearly 40%. In the realm of public demonstrations, over half of Gen Z (51%) have participated in rallies or protests to support specific causes or social issues, with a slight increase to 56% observed among those in higher ed.[51]

49. Ibid.

50. Twenge, Jean. (2023) "Monitoring the Future: Depressive Symptoms in US 8th, 10th, and 12th Graders"

51. United Way of the National Capital Area. (2024, March 5) Blog: "The Gen Z Activism Survey". https://unitedwaynca.org/blog/gen-z-activism-survey/

Made in the USA
Middletown, DE
27 April 2025